Fifty-S[...]
Pieces
of the
Cloudcroft
Puzzle

...Some Secrets of the Sacramento Mountains, and
other New Mexico Law Enforcement Stories...

TO: SHRT
REMEMBERING THE GOOD
TIMES AT AJAS!

Billy Anders

Billy Anders

outskirtspress
DENVER, COLORADO

This book is dedicated to the citizens of the Sacramento Mountains, who have both fed bacon to me and saved my bacon. You're the best. I know you'll always honor and protect the memory of Deputy Sheriff Robert Hedman Jr., who gave his all for you. Below is his last known image, taken two weeks before he was killed on December 18, 2004. It reflects his true cowboy nature, his real comfort zone.

Rest in peace, Bob. You are not forgotten.

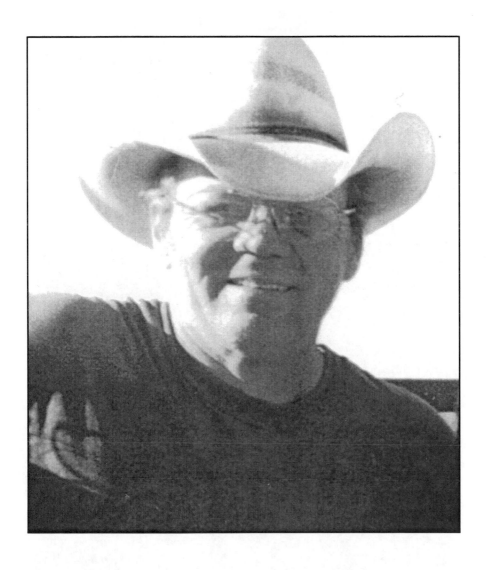

Table of Contents

Acknowledgments ...i
Foreword ... ii

1. I Got the Message, Little Cloudcroft Lady....................................1
2. Life Too Frantic? Let's Go To A Quiet Place…5
3. Bubba Done Up and Flew Away...9
4. The Ups and Downs of Mountain Cows13
5. Standing on the Thin Blue Line ...17
6. Reuniting With Those From Our Past.................................22
7. A Good Man Who Lived on a Small Hill25
8. Thanksgiving Is For the Birds...27
9. Keeping Our Promises To A True Man of the West32
10. The Year of the Boat...37
11. I Hate Wintertime in Cloudcroft41
12. The Little Black Trailer – Saving Money in a Tough Economy ..44
13. Moondog Moretti, Trains, Neil Mitchell, and Other Things......48
14. Hey Ma! Thinking of You…Hope You're Still Dancin'!53
15. Dam It! A Revolutionary Water Ride that Hurt So Good..........58
16. When Tony the Tagger Tagged the Tunnel of Love63
17. Jane, May Your Future Travels Be On Happy Highways!68
18. Sure, Get Your Kicks on Route 66, But Never
 Feel Blue on Highway 82! ...72

19. O' Christmas Tree – Time to Gas Up the Bow Saw!77

20. To Sail On the GYPSY WIND…..82

21. Part II, Voyage of the GYPSY WIND!.................................86

22. Gotta Go Gotta Go Gotta Go Right Now!............................91

23. Welcome To the Real World! ...96

24. Way to Go, George Collins! ...101

25. Independence Day Reflections on the Coming of Independence..105

26. The Soldier on the Mantle ...109

27. Remembering the Veterans from the Land of Bad Things113

28. A Dark Christmas Story: The Secret War
 of Cowboy Bob and the Posse ...118

29. Cloudcroft Love, Like an Old-Fashioned Phone Call124

30. For Valentine's Day, Everything You Wanted to Know
 about True Love in Cloudcroft, and …129

31. There's a Small New Star in the Western Sky........................133

32. The Day of the Broom ...138

33. Linc'ing Up and Re-Joyce'ing With Friends in North Carolina..143

34. The True Story of the Train That Saved a Space Shuttle...........148

35. "The Art of Racing in the Rain", a book review by Sara Lee ...152

36. Welcome to the Mountains! Snow Driving 101….....................157

37. A Cloudcroft Christmas is a Very Good Thing.......................162

38. Happy New Year! Looking Back to Look at the Future............166

39. Of Jerry Heinzelmann, Village Hardware
 and Nancy Nice the Cat ...170

40. Slipping and Sliding on the Casino Freeway............................175

41. Cloudcroft to the Atlantic Ocean! Swan Song of the Shasta....180

42. Brother, Can You Spare a Dollar (Store)?.............................186

43. Horsing Around With the Pain-In-The-Neck Board191

44. A Working Visit to Chama and the Cumbres &
 Toltec Scenic Railroad ...196

45. Listening to the Hoofbeats of Extraordinary Lives..................201

46. Where You Are, There Let Me Stay206

47. A New Year, A New Path, A New Beginning210

48. A Classic Cloudcroft Confrontation: Little Angel
 vs. Little Devil...215
49. The Night Johnny Lost Sue on U. S. Highway 82...................220
50. Some Secrets of the Sacramentos ...224
51. In New Mexico, These Are a Few of My Favorite Things.........228
52. Thanksgiving – A Time to Remember Health Care Workers ...232
53. A Cloudcroft Christmas Trip ..239
54. A Very Humane Thought for the New Year..............................243
55. Protecting and Serving, 24/7. Who You Gonna Call,
 Ghostbusters? ..248
56. In April, Thoughts Turn to Flights of Fancy
 in a Cloudzoni 101 ...253
57. You've Gotta Know When to Hold 'em,
 Know When to Fold 'em... ...258

Epilogue...263

Acknowledgments

Thanks to the former owners and editors of the Cloudcroft Mountain Monthly, Gary and Gloria Wood; and the current owner and publisher, Darrell Pehr, for giving me a newspaper voice through 'Pieces of the Puzzle' from 2006 through 2015. Your generosity over those nine years is appreciated!

Also thanks to the many Mountain Monthly staff with whom I worked. You couldn't have been more supportive! Deadlines? We didn't need no stinking deadlines! Forgive me for always pushing the limit.

My love always to Cynthia, my wife, for tolerating the keyboard time; and my humble thanks to the Good Lord for giving me the ability to either think straight or to fake it.

Without readers, all this is pointless. Thank you, good people, you are truly appreciated!

Foreword

My wife and I married in 1993 and honeymooned in Cloudcroft, New Mexico. We'd planned to vacation in the Pocono Mountains of Pennsylvania but changed our destination on the advice of a friend. It was our first visit to the Sacramento Mountains.

Over a week in early December that year, we were smitten. Not just with each other, but with Cloudcroft too. There was an unexpected gentle six inch snowfall. It was peaceful, beautiful.

Over the next three years, we visited several more times during various seasons. Deciding to retire from our jobs in San Antonio, Texas – she as an educator, me as a police officer – we toured other small towns in Arizona and New Mexico to confirm our choice of a new home. Cloudcroft remained at the top of the list.

There was just something very appealing about this up high yet down to earth spot in the Sacramentos at almost 9,000 feet elevation!

In the village one summer day after we'd just left 108 degree weather in Texas, when the temperature on the Cloudcroft Boardwalk was only 70, we learned that the Cloudcroft High School counselor's job was

open. Cynthia, my wife, applied and was hired. She would serve in that capacity from 1996 – 2004.

She loved her job and her students, and did good work. In a proclamation signed by Governor Bill Richardson in 2004, she was honored as the State of New Mexico's high school counselor of the year.

During 1997, I became a police officer in Ruidoso Downs for one year, then worked for the Otero County Sheriff's Office for seven more as a mountain deputy. Our home was in Cloudcroft. My job was a dream come true! Nearly perfect, at the perfect time in my life.

Into every life, of course, rain must fall. It's the nature of human existence.

The following quote is from my book, A Cop's Prison Letters to Cloudcroft, published in 2009.

"On December 18, 2004, about 7:00 PM, Deputy Sheriff Robert Hedman and I were dispatched to a house about five miles east of Cloudcroft, New Mexico, for a report of shots fired, accompanied by an argument. A domestic violence call, one of the most dangerous in law enforcement.

It was dark, a cold night. Just after we arrived, Deputy Hedman was ambushed in the dark and killed at the back door, shot in the head at close range by an assailant who had just murdered his girlfriend. She was eight months pregnant. The unborn child died as well. He had stuffed the pregnant woman's body into a sleeping bag, dumped her into a closet. The woman's distraught three year old child had been wounded by a bullet or wood that had fragmented when hit by a bullet.

After making a quick radio call, I was surprised too - ambushed - near the front door, in the dark, from a distance of four or five feet. The .357 Magnum bullet grazed my left arm as I returned fire. The same

assailant had the child, a little girl, standing in front of him. I fired four rounds. A short time later I fired a controversial fifth shot. Sometime during or after the five shots I fired, the assailant died.

In such a situation, I was trained to shoot back until the threat was over, the action was stopped. But those in authority felt I had fired the fifth shot in the 'heat of passion'. I was charged with voluntary manslaughter."

I digress from the earlier book to say this: The immediate issue of saving the child was paramount to every decision, to every action taken by Bob and me. At the defining moment, not much else mattered. Help was a long way away. Then, it was also critical to get medical help to Bob, to see if he might be saved. In the final analysis, the little girl did survive.

Back to A Cop's Prison Letters to Cloudcroft.

"Faced with a much harsher possible federal sentence, I reluctantly chose to plead guilty to the state charge as an offered alternative. Had I not done so, I faced these possibilities: Bankruptcy; a prison stay of two to three years awaiting trial while incarcerated; being tried in the northern part of New Mexico instead of the area where I live; a sentence of 15 years or more if convicted on another charge; perhaps others.

Had I been a younger man, a richer man, a more stubborn man, not a family man - I may have chosen differently. What would you have done?

The community of Cloudcroft, New Mexico, where I lived and worked, was supportive. That's a gross understatement. In 31 years of law enforcement, I'd never seen anything like it. Aside from the outward demonstration of love and concern, citizens raised more than $60,000.00 through direct donations, auctions, garage sales, collection jars in businesses. They paid my legal fees.

I left home for New Mexico's maximum security prison at Santa Fe on March 10, 2006, facing one year in confinement. Our Cloudcroft newspaper, The Mountain Monthly, allowed me to write a letter home each issue, describing the prison experience. People had promised to write me, to stay in touch.

Letters from home would be a very important part of my survival. I knew that and I wanted them. I also understood a fact of life: Out of sight, out of mind. So, selfishly, I hoped that a monthly letter from me would serve to keep busy people reminded of my status.

Quickly I realized that describing the day to day things I saw and heard in prison would be difficult. To have honestly done so, I might have angered someone in authority, might not have been released early on 'good time'. It's not a nice place. So I chose to write about personal and law enforcement experiences, with a Cloudcroft connection whenever possible.

While in prison for 10 months, I received mail Monday through Friday. Some days I received as many as 20 letters and cards. It was astounding. Mail clerks weren't always happy with me. I would divide the mail to have something to read on Saturdays and Sundays. Mail from home was a key component of my successful prison stay.

I was humbled. People wrote me who had more serious problems than I did. Some of them had life-threatening medical issues. Some of them have since passed away.

After my release, I returned to Cloudcroft and was invited to continue the column I was writing. In July 2007 I was asked to name it and chose 'Pieces of the Puzzle'.

To me, life is like that. Each experience or piece of knowledge helps complete our own puzzle, a sometimes complicated picture that isn't finalized until the centerpiece of our personal puzzle falls into place

with our last breath. And law enforcement work in a small community such as ours constantly turned up another piece of the local puzzle. Who was related, what past events had taken place that affected the current one, etc.

It isn't my nature to express my emotions and feelings openly. But Cloudcroft, New Mexico, and the surrounding communities bared their souls for me. Why shouldn't I bare mine in return? Thus the stories I've written have often been very personal. Sometimes, having written them, I've hesitated to submit them. For example, dealing with the recent deaths of my parents. But finally I've relented. Why not? The community gave me its heart and soul. They gave me back my life. What else could I do?

I'm not a preacher, don't want to be. The Bible holds preachers to a higher standard and I have enough trouble with the regular one. But my Christian beliefs were invaluable in helping me survive prison. I'll admit I'm glad to have had the help. I promised God that I would try to repay His blessings. You'll see He is mentioned, at least in a subtle way, in almost every article. That's no accident. I'm just giving credit where credit is due."

The Mountain Monthly column, 'Pieces of the Puzzle', continued for nine years, through June 2015. Eighty more stories were written in addition to those previously published in A Cop's Prison Letters to Cloudcroft. This book contains 57 of those, selected as best representing what I believe Cloudcroft, New Mexico, is all about; and what it and law enforcement mean to me.

This effort is primarily intended to preserve these accounts for family and friends, but I certainly welcome other readers.

Whether you live in Cloudcroft now, or would like to, I hope you find these tales helpful to understand the nature of the little village we love to call home!

Burro Street in Cloudcroft, New Mexico, 2015. Business district and main thoroughfare.

1

I Got the Message, Little Cloudcroft Lady

November 2008

Sometimes small women scare me.

Other women scare me sometimes, too, but small women especially scare me.

Sitting in a Cloudcroft café recently, calmly eating breakfast, I was approached by a small Cloudcroft woman. She walked directly to me, purposefully, a small woman on a mission. There were tears in her eyes. Uh oh.

"Billy Anders, I'm mad at you. I'm never reading your column again. You've made me cry for the last time. First it was your dog, Cookie. Then your Mom. Now your step-dad, Don. I'm tired of you writing about people and a dog dying. I got up this morning and read about your step-dad. Now I'll be sad all day."

My first inclination, she was kidding. My second inclination, she was not. And my second one arrived pretty quickly.

So I promised I wouldn't write about death anytime soon, that my next article would be light-hearted, hopefully even funny. One can always hope. She promised to read again, if I'd keep my promise.

She caused me to reflect on other small women who've previously scared me. There've been quite a few.

Once I was pulling a small trailer to Texas to pick up a boat. A small boat. The trailer had little eight inch wheels. I was between Hope, a very small place, and Artesia. I was doing 68 MPH in the dreaded 55 MPH zone. A small mistake, what?

I met a New Mexico State Police officer who turned around and stopped me. It was a Two Pillow Cop. (That size comes in both the Man and Woman model.) A One Pillow Cop can see over the dashboard but under the top part of the steering wheel by sitting on one pillow. With two pillows, they can see over the steering wheel.

Of course I'm for equal opportunity but I worry for those Pillow Cops' safety. I remember the huge thugs I encountered during my police career. But who can argue with political correctness?

This one was a small Woman model. Recognizing her as someone whom I'd met on-duty once at an accident scene in Eddy County, I relaxed.

"Yep, guilty. Sorry, I'm in a hurry, running late. And if the speed limit was 90, I'd still have been doing just 68. Wouldn't want those little trailer wheels to turn any faster," I said.

Well, no citation, but she bluntly said: "You'd better slow your butt down, mister!" So much for friendship and the thin blue line. "Yes, ma'am." I saluted smartly and drove away. Small women with big guns always scare me and she had a big gun.

Another example. Stopping a very small local elderly woman - she was

at least 80 - one day for speeding, she uttered those famous words. "Why are you harassing me? Why aren't you out there doing your job, catching bank robbers? You s?#@ of a ?>)&%#*! Leave me alone, you rotten %$|^||%$|!!"

Holy cow. Remembering I'd handled several deaths and many serious injuries in traffic accidents and none in bank robberies - I couldn't even remember anyone getting hurt by slipping on a wet floor at the bank - I tried to explain that. Didn't work. "Well, I don't give a $#%@ about that. Just leave me alone, you &^|%$||%|^|!"

She was a scary small woman. I knew how a sailor sometimes feels.

A further example. Another small local woman was driving too fast, past the James Canyon Church. Seventy-something. Her speed, not her age, although they were close. I knew her. "Hello, Mrs. A. Nonymous. How are you? Do you have an emergency today?"

She was nice. "No, Billy, but I was just down to the eye doctor in Alamogordo, had my eyes dilated. I can't see a thing. I'm just in a hurry to get to my house." Good grief! What a unique reason for speeding, and another small woman who scared me. I saw that she got home safely, no ticket.

My final scary small woman story today. My canoe partner, Les, and I were in West Texas. We planned to paddle down the Pecos River through very isolated country to the Rio Grande. At a river road cross-ing, very stern warning signs were posted. No Trespassing. Violators Will Be Shot On Sight. That sort of thing.

In most cases, a navigable river is a public river. If you can paddle a boat down it, you can use it. But old Spanish land grants put property lines at the center of the river. The ranchers whose families have held title since those days see it that way. They believe they own the river or at least half of it. Thus the signs we saw.

I told Les: "Hey, we're good guys. I'm a cop. You're a fireman. Let's talk to the rancher and ask permission. We don't leave anything but footprints."

We knocked. A very small elderly Texas ranch lady answered. A lady accustomed to dealing with rattlesnakes and coyotes, by herself when necessary. A Winchester .30-.30 was in sight near her right hand. We asked if we might put our boat in the river. Her reply: "Sonny, you see those signs? They mean just what they say." She glanced towards the rifle.

Again I saluted smartly, said: "Yes, ma'am." We left quickly, invoked Plan B, drove to Amistad Lake, camped out, paddled around. But my friend Les is a self-described hardheaded Dutchman. A couple of months later he returned with another paddling buddy, snuck into the Pecos River at midnight at the signs, paddled to the Rio Grande.

Les noticed, though, that a mysterious rider, smaller size, on a larger size horse, shadowed them from a distance for two or three days. A small rider with a saddle gun. Was it her? Probably not, but then again…

Yes, small women scare me sometimes. It's like they're larger than life. Little Cloudcroft lady, are you reading this? Do you see I've kept my promise? Whew.

May the Good Lord protect us from all danger, including small women who mean what they say.

2

Life Too Frantic?
Let's Go To A Quiet Place...

February 2009

February. A quiet month. The grip of winter, a time for huggin'. Well, that kind too, but specifically heater huggin'. Also a time for thinking, contemplating. Getting ready for the new year, for spring, for summer.

For serious thinking, we need a Quiet Place. Often our home doesn't work. At mine, I'm distracted by LSTD. Lotta Stuff To Do. Things that keep me from the best sort of concentrated thought.

So...every now and then I head for a Quiet Place, a real one. Do you have such a place? When I used to jog or walk long distances, often the Quiet Place was just in my head. Not much else to do, the athletics involved are simple. Jog or walk. Meanwhile - think, plan, organize.

I'm a sociable person, but occasionally solitude seems necessary. When I worked for the sheriff's office, I had some special Quiet Places in the Sacramento Mountains. Prisoners weren't the only ones who sometimes felt the need to escape. Every few weeks I'd pack a sack lunch,

head down Highway 130...turn up Upper Rio Penasco Road, then climb Prestridge Hill towards Hay Canyon.

Topping the mountain, I'd pull over, exit the truck, inhale the fresh air, look closely at the beautiful view of Hay Canyon over and below. Just enjoy the sight, alone. Later - normally no traffic to disturb you there - drive over into the canyon, turn right. A few hundred yards up is a very nice spring.

Sgt Jeff Farmer introduced me to that spring years ago. Arriving, I'd fill a bottle with fresh water, find a pull off, enjoy my lunch. Quietly. A good thinking spot, there in the peace and isolation of upper Hay Canyon. Just sitting on the pickup tailgate.

In the almost 4,000 square miles of the sheriff's mountain district, there are Quiet Places aplenty. An additional favorite was Hornbuckle Hill. Ever been there? It's just a mile off Timberon Road on that end of Westside Road. I'd stop at the top of Hornbuckle Hill, listen to the wind, quietly search the view. See Bug Scuffle Ranch in the near distance.

If I'd had eagle eyes, maybe I could have seen the city limit signs of El Paso and Las Cruces. Okay, I said maybe...

Before the mountains, I lived in San Antonio, Texas. A big Noisy Place. When things got too hectic, sometimes I'd fly my little airplane up to 10,000 feet above the city, reduce the city to postage-stamp size. There, San Antonio, take that!

The cockpit was a nice mental Quiet Place, really put what seemed like big problems into their proper perspective. Nobody but me up there. But I really was just the copilot; it made me remember who the real Pilot is.

Where's your all-time favorite Quiet Place? Mine is a couple of states

away. It's a little church and cemetery in the Mississippi countryside. My great grandparents donated the land around 1900. I don't believe doing so, by itself, got them to heaven. But it was a good work, and I appreciate what they did.

I like to go there alone, or at least with someone who doesn't say much. Entering our row, I visit first with Aunt Myrt, my favorite great aunt who had a wonderful sense of humor. I learned from her. Then there's stoic Uncle Chris, we played checkers. Uncle Motor, my dad called him, because he moved so slowly. More great aunts and uncles, a cousin. Next, my great grandparents and grandparents.

Holding down the end spot are my mother and father, my mother a recent arrival. It's such a very Quiet Place, it seems an unlikely spot for her. She wasn't always a Quiet Person.

I'm sad for a bit, I miss them all. But I think private thoughts of happier times, remember what they did for me, what they stood for. Consider how I can do a better job of living up to their teachings. It helps me focus.

I recall that the family of my partner and friend, Deputy Bob Hedman, unselfishly gave me some of his ashes for this favorite Quiet Place. I discussed it with my mother then. She agreed, without hesitation.

Imagine - Bob, a New Yorker - in a Mississippi cemetery. But that's a good thing. Winter, spring, summer, fall…he's part of us now. "Watch your back here, Bob," I think. "My mother will be playing tricks on you."

Time to go. I glance eastward. Just a few yards away stood my ancestral home. The home of my great grandparents. Bits of red brick are still scattered amongst the pine trees. From the old two story house that burned during the Great Depression. Accidental? Well…it was about to be lost to the bank. The economy, you know. There was a $5,000

insurance policy. Family lore has it "someone" burned it to keep the home from being repossessed.

Great grandparents Wilford and Fannie Robinson's home in Peoria, Mississippi, destroyed by fire in the 1930s.

My dad was about 20 at the time, a rounder. He never admitted being an arsonist. But I imagine I hear a familiar chuckle as I leave. It kind of puts life back on track. As I depart my Quiet Place, my favorite one, I soon begin to feel rejuvenated. Moving away from the yesterdays and hopefully distant tomorrows. Better ready for the world, the todays.

Thanks for going with me, and for being quiet. I hope you can visit your Quiet Place soon, if you need to. May God bless you with a quiet kind of peace there.

3

Bubba Done Up and Flew Away

April 2009

He was a big man. He stood 6'4" tall, weighed 260 or more. He was also a quiet man. If not quiet, at least a man of few words. He wouldn't use 10 or 20 if one or two would do.

Some said he was sometimes gruff. I didn't see that, just saw a man who didn't say much. He was a law-abiding person, but I saw and appreciated him most as a rule-breaker.

For years he served his community, you and me. He worked for his water district in Twin Forks, a tough job. If you had looked up "fire and EMS volunteer" in the dictionary, you'd have seen his picture. He served the James Canyon VFD faithfully. He didn't miss a bell.

There was an accident a few years ago 16 miles east of Mayhill. Seven people were killed, including six young teenage girls. It was the kind of event that causes people to rethink their volunteer role, and some didn't return. But he persevered through that kind of thing. He kept his feet solidly on the line.

Last December, I heard he had cancer. Two months to live. I sent him a letter. 'You were there for us," I wrote, "now I'm here for you. Please call me when I can help."

Typical of him, he didn't call, but I went to see him a couple of times. On one occasion I helped a mutual friend of ours move his bed. That was it. Many more did much more.

A rule-breaker? You see, on December 18, 2004, when my law enforcement partner and friend was shot, and we both needed help, he and four others came. Quickly, no hesitation. The rule said the scene had to be safe, secure. It wasn't. But he and the others came anyway. At great risk to their lives. He didn't say much, but he was there. He broke the rule, and I appreciated that. If my friend could have been saved, he would have seen to it.

Again that night he saw things that would have caused anyone to reconsider the volunteer job. But he continued to serve.

When I visited him the first time recently, when he was very ill, I stupidly tried to say something light-hearted. He lived on Blue Jay Trail. "I've never seen even one blue jay on this street. Have you?" I asked. I was just trying to perk him up a little. This man of few words had the perfect one-word answer. "Several," he responded. I had no cute reply.

Once he was riding his four-wheeler on his water district job and discovered an open second floor door, evidence of a burglary. He would have gotten a ladder, but I made a risky climb up and over the high railing. I could read the following on his face, as he waited in the yard: "You idiot. You're gonna break your neck. What do you think you're doing? Guess I'll have to stick around and patch you up or call for more help when you fall. Good grief!"

"Hang around, will you, until I get up here, and get a downstairs door unlocked?" I asked. The reply, instead of the above, from the man of

few words: "I'm here." And I knew he would be so long as I needed him.

He worked for years at the Tonopah Test Range facility in Nevada. Sandia National Laboratories conducts research there. It's where the F-117 Stealth fighter was developed. His family said many of his friends and co-workers also came down with cancer. They believe it was due to the nature of their work. So we owe him additional gratitude for what he did for our country long before he got to Cloudcroft.

Wonder if disputes occur in heaven? One angel pulling another's wing, something like that? Because of his dedication to service, I can imagine him being tasked by God to settle such things. "Get over there to Cloud 17 and take care of it," God might say. This new angel of unnecessary words would probably just reply: "Yes sir."

God, I doubt you'll take a mere mortal's advice but please don't ask him about blue jays and expect a long conversation.

My second and last visit with him was just a few days before he passed away. He was very weak, and I had to lean over to catch his words. I could only make out one: "...................appreciate...........," he whispered. I believe he tried to tell me he appreciated my coming. I could only tell him thank you and God bless.

I missed his memorial service at the Mayhill Baptist Church, was in Texas with a broke-down car. I wanted to be at the church and I'm sorry I wasn't.

Alamogordo Hospice helped him and his family in his last days. He helped me and you, especially the citizens who lived anywhere east of Cloudcroft, all his days here. If he didn't put out your house fire or transport you to the hospital, he was prepared and ready to do so. Will you join me in sending a donation to Hospice in his memory?

It's: Alamogordo Hospice, 1859 Indian Wells Road, Alamogordo NM 88310. Thank you.

Some called him Bubba. I guess he liked that, he had a license plate with that name. I knew him only as Jim. Jimmy Wayne Shores, August 30, 1939 to February 25, 2009, not long enough.

Appreciated you, Jim. Bubba Angel.

4

The Ups and Downs
of Mountain Cows

May 2009

In San Juan Capistrano, California, the swallows come home every year, on or about the 17th of March. They winter in Argentina, then fly back to that old California mission in the spring to build their mud nests. They're about as regular as clockwork. They return to South America in October.

Do we have anything comparable in or near Cloudcroft? Well, we have cows. Our cows come home around the first of May to graze peacefully in the "high country" along the rim of the Sacramentos. California's swallows number in the thousands. We probably have a few hundred cows. But cows make up in quality what they lose in numbers.

Ever had a swallow burger or tried to drink swallow milk? I'm told the meat is grainy and the milk has a muddy taste. Like a catfish that's eaten too soon when caught.

The Forest Service allows ranchers with permits to graze their cattle on

forest land for the six months of summer. So cows have to - figuratively at least - pack their bags in the fall. They go downhill around October, a swallow-like schedule. Most mountain cows go to winter pasturage in the Tularosa Basin. Not exactly Argentina, but I'll bet the sunsets are prettier.

Annually in the fall, you'll be reminded of the cows' pilgrimage as you slowly follow their trailers down the mountain. Cows are heavier than swallows, at least in equal numbers, and ranchers have to drive carefully going off the "hill". Cows' wings are seriously underdeveloped, and they can't fly, so they're dependent on human transportation.

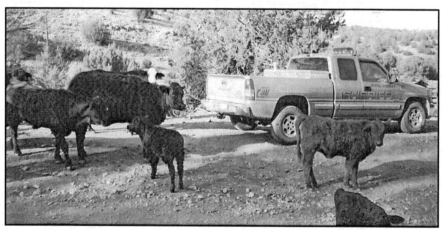

Elk Canyon cows hoping for a hay handout during a forest fire in 2002.

Once while I was in law enforcement here, there was a traffic accident just below the tunnel on Highway 82 with a load of cows involved. None were injured, but their trailer was tilted at a crazy angle. The cows weren't happy, and I felt sorry for them. Did I unbolt their trailer door, let them loose and have to gather them up later - or let them suffer in fright? I was - yes - on the horns of a dilemma.

If I'd been in a similar situation, and a cow had meandered by, I would have bellowed out: "Unlock the door!" So I unlocked theirs. The relieved cows got out, walked around, relaxed somewhat. "Got milk?"

they inquired, in the sense that grateful victims released from their ordeal have asked many times. "We'll send you some." Alas, as with previous statements I'd heard, this one dried up too. The only free milk I ever got was using the extra stamp from Allsup's.

Were our migrating cows ever crime victims? Oh yes. The grazing wasn't always so peaceful. We all know how cows look so much like deer or elk, so unfortunately they were sometimes shot with arrows, even bullets, by a very few irresponsible hunters. Two bow hunters near Telephone Canyon, thoroughly hidden in the woods in camouflage, laughingly shot a cow with an arrow. The cow wandered away, presumably to die. It was never found.

How was this crime discovered? Unknown to the thoroughly hidden bow hunters, another even more thoroughly hidden bow hunter was about 30 yards away - deep in the grass - and saw the whole thing. They were from different hunting camps, and the witness remembered that others knew where he was hunting. He remained concealed, but thinking he might get blamed, he later came forward. Cruelty To An Animal of the nature committed had just changed to a felony about two weeks before. Oops.

Another cow, off Benson Ridge Road, walked around with an arrow in its side for months. The owner eventually caught her, removed the arrow. That lucky cow survived. We went to great lengths to identify the arrow's owner but couldn't do so. Maybe it was the person who "shot an arrow into the air, it fell to earth, he knew not where". Maybe it happened on New Year's Eve, at midnight.

A small calf was shot and killed by a rifle bullet just off Road 64, towards Timberon, near the Sacramento Lookout fire tower. Another cow was killed in the same manner off Russia Canyon Road. I should add that the great majority of hunters don't do these sort of things. If any cows are readers, they're breathing a sigh of relief now.

Ever milked a cow? As a youngster, I learned how at my grandparents' farm in Mississippi. Guess I was just a squirt. The cows got milked at 4:30 AM. Holy cow, that's early. About twice a year, I had a little fun by sneaking in after my grandparents' bedtime and resetting the clock two hours fast. If it was bad for the cows to have cold human hands on their you-know-whats at 4:30 AM, imagine the same thing at 2:30 AM! Not contented cows, I assure you.

A few years ago, I was alone at an abandoned house just above Bridal Veil Falls, along the Cloud Climbing Railroad route below High Rolls, investigating a vandalism call. Hearing a loud crashing noise inside a small outbuilding, I imagined "bear!" and cautiously walked over. Hesitantly, I peeked through a crack in the door. Remember the scene in the movie where King Kong looks at Jessica Lange through a window of the Empire State Building? His giant eyes?

Huge eyes like that were looking right back at me just a couple inches away. Cowabunga, dude! Instinctively I jumped back, then when the bear mooed, I realized what had nosed inside, gotten trapped. This cow had apparently passed the time by baking. Judging by the number of pies she'd left there, it'd been several days. I removed the door's hinges to free her. Immediately she headed for the bovine version of Jamocha Bean, the creek in the canyon bottom. She was a thirsty girl.

If you're a lady who thinks your Mountain Man is an unromantic cuss when, instead of giving you candy or flowers, he says: "Honey, I'll love you 'til the cows come home," ...just remember, to him the cows have always come home and always will, spring after spring after spring. So maybe that's not such a bad thing to hear. In his mind, he means forever.

May God bless our mountain cows and keep them safe. And good luck to the swallows too. That's a lot of flying.

5

Standing on the Thin Blue Line

August 2009

Passing through Albuquerque recently, I learned that Sgt Joe Harris of the Sandoval County Sheriff's Office had just been killed in a shootout. He and a partner were staking out remote mountain cabins near NM Highway 126. That road runs from Cuba to Los Alamos.

Sgt Harris and his partner encountered an armed burglar known as the Cookie Bandit. That part of Sandoval County is remarkably similar to the Cloudcroft area.

Having just driven through Cuba, I'd glanced at the NM Highway 126 turnoff. About four years ago, I elected not to drive that road due to very heavy rain and mud. Had I done so then and gotten stuck, would it have been Sgt Joe Harris who came to my rescue? Perhaps.

This trip, I'd just had breakfast at a Cuba restaurant. But on leaving northbound, I saw two police cars at another café. Darn! Should I have waited? The cops always know where the best food and pretty girls are. Was one of the officers inside Sgt Joe Harris?

North of town, a Sandoval County Sheriff's Office vehicle had a car stopped. Could this instead have been Sgt Joe Harris?

God knows, if any of those cars had been that of Sgt Joe Harris, and I had known what was to come, I would have stopped and said: "Thank you, Joe, for standing on the thin blue line for us."

Police uniforms are traditionally blue in color, but the thin line can be brown, tan, green or black. It's still the same line. The one that protects you – the good – from evil.

The most dangerous city in the world is less than 100 miles away! Juarez, Mexico. People are murdered by the double digits each day. Do you recall there are only three or four thin blue lines between Cloudcroft and Juarez?

I remember officers who fell while standing on the line. James Anderson, who died in 1975, shot by a barricaded person. I flew a helicopter that day, delivering ammo to the scene. Anderson Park at Medina Lake, Texas, is named for James. I've told my son – a San Antonio sergeant now - I don't want an Anders Park. He's been in two shootings in 12 years, but I'm proud of him for being out there on the line. I just ask God to keep him safe.

Eloy Gonzales was shot and killed in 1977. I took Eloy's place in a police squad in San Antonio, Texas, after his death. It seemed his comrades were a little angry with me, almost as if I was partly responsible for his loss. But they soon came around when they saw I would stand with them.

Bernabe Salazar, 1978. Bernie was killed in my district. Shot by a drug addict in a wheelchair. I had been tasked that day to watch over a city council meeting, wasn't close. But I told the council: "Gotta go. Now!"

Gilbert Ramirez, killed Christmas Eve, 1988. A one in a million shot

by a drunk, but it happened. Christmas was forever changed for his family.

Ed Gorrell, standing the line near the Alamo, 1988. Close to where the line was drawn in the sand by Colonel William Travis in 1836. If Ed had been there with the colonel, he would have crossed that line with the defenders. I'll never forget seeing his wife and little girl at the Police Officer Memorial ceremony on the grounds of the US Capitol, Washington, DC, in 1989. Just sitting there crying in the rain.

And, Dennis Goeble in 1991. In uniform, having lunch, properly facing the door. The assailant approached from behind, shot him in the head, but escaped death row. His attorney convinced the jury Dennis was off duty since he was on a meal break. Good grief.

One of the toughest for me was Fabian Dominguez, January 15, 1995. He was a good looking redheaded kid, I was the commander of his substation. He'd had a rough start in West Texas, but found his calling. Fabian had a beautiful wife and delightful two year old twin girls. He left two hours early that Sunday morning after working all night, to attend church, to teach Sunday School. Two blocks from home, he encountered burglars, stealing guns. He knew the people he saw didn't live there. He could have gone by. But he was standing the thin blue line. Going by wasn't an option.

I went to his home, told his wife. Oh my. Those little twins are big twins now, 16 years of age. I hope they're well and know of their dad's courage. I do. Fabian Dominguez State Jail, part of the Texas Department of Corrections, is named for him. I still remember Fabian's wonderful smile.

Of course, my partner and friend, Deputy Bob Hedman, killed December 18, 2004. You know that story. Bob accompanied me on stakeouts like the one at which Sgt Joe Harris was killed. I remember one in Twin Forks, because of repeated vandalism there. We called in

10-7, off duty, but by prearrangement remained concealed in the bushes. Luckily, no Cookie Bandit was out and about that night.

Later, Bob wasn't so fortunate. But he always took his place in the line. It was my honor and privilege to stand the thin line with him.

Would anyone take on this crazy job now? Amazingly, yes. This past May, I addressed the Southwestern NM Law Enforcement Academy Class, 17 cadets, in Hobbs. Told about the shooting incident I was involved in, gave them information that might help them later. They invited me to graduation on June 11, 2009. What a thrill! For a little while, I was back on the line. I was the Ole Sarge, they were my troopers. Together we could do this world some good!

Each has unique skills. Daniel Markham of Alamogordo sang, wonderfully. David Rodriguez of Artesia, a concert musician with a Master's degree, has taught, performed with a symphony orchestra. "Carry that guitar with you, David," I told him. "You just might save some young person with it." Rudy Fields of Alamogordo is inspired by a grandfather who was a cop. Rudy, with a winning personality, will be a good one. Another young man was a missionary's son.

Since attending my daughter's athletic events there, I've always been a little apprehensive about being in Loving. But now Tyler Knight will be on duty, and he'll keep us Cloudcroft Bears safe. I believe that.

Dagoberto Rodriguez of Clovis. So shy. But one of several veterans of Iraq duty. Been there, done that. There were two outstanding young women – Cathy Carnes of Hobbs; and Carolee Jones – a former US Marine- of Portales. Her dad is a friend of mine.

Robert Blanchard, Nate Clay, Bryan Generotzky – Bryan 50 years old, formerly a Hobbs officer, coming back for more. Daniel Gonzales, Jason Herrera, Ryan Rodriguez, Jacob Sanchez. Then

Chad Scroggins, Jacob Sernas, finally Pete Vargas. Representing Roswell, Vaughn, Carlsbad and Tucumcari as well.

The thin blue line may be thin, but it's still out there, thanks to good people like those above. Outstanding people. We'll sleep well while they watch over us, as Sgt Joe Harris of Sandoval County watched. It's Joe's turn now to sleep, with the angels. Thank you, Sgt Harris, for a life well lived.

May God bless and comfort his family. And may they know that Cloudcroft appreciates Joe having bravely stood on the thin blue line for all us New Mexicans.

6

Reuniting With Those From Our Past

September 2009

Reunions come in many shapes and sizes. We're probably most familiar with high school class reunions. It seems that some people love them, while others hate them.

The 10 year high school reunion could be the most significant. By then, the Friday night hero's knees are acting up, the bright lights of the football field have faded. But the nerd – the guy who played in the band or – horrors, sang in the choir - may have become a software genius.

At my 10 year event, such was the case. Gene was limping, selling real estate. But Jack had developed computer expertise, grown curly hair, was sort of a Bill Gates clone. And his BMW attracted the ladies' attention. Poor Gene's pickup was hidden in the shadows. Back in school, Jack hadn't been able to get a date for the prom. Gene had taken a cheerleader, of course.

Military units have reunions. Navy veterans, for example, take pride in meeting with their old shipmates. I've written about my stepfather's visits with his WWII buddies from the USS Memphis, a cruiser; about Reg Duncan's later year sorties with his friends from the USS Zeilin, the Mighty Z. Both my stepdad and Reg, regrettably, are now gone, have attended their last reunions on this good earth.

There are family reunions, of course. My mother's family meets annually in June, in Mississippi. She was one of nine children. There's only a sister and a brother left. But those get-togethers continue and I'll keep attending. At least we can look at photos, have great remembrances. And it's great to see Aunt Marjorie and Uncle Bert and all my cousins.

Some reunions are marked by not who's there, but who's not there. In East Texas, I flew small airplanes commercially one year. I'd look below me and see crop duster pilots dodging power lines and antennas. Later, as a police helicopter pilot, I faced those same enemies – wires and antennas. Once a guy wire attached to an antenna got mixed up with the setting sun, and I nearly snagged it. The guy wire, not the sun. Just a bit too exciting.

Anyway, I've heard that duster pilots always first look around at their conventions and meetings to see who's not there and not to see who's there. Who did the wire or antenna get this time?

Some reunions are smaller in numbers and are nice. An older Cloudcroft couple had been boyfriend and girlfriend in high school but each later married someone else. After 50 or so years, their respective spouses had died. The surviving spouses found each other, reunited in marriage. A happy marriage, incidentally, judging by how they look at each other when I see them. That's a nice reunion.

A buddy of mine from the San Antonio, Texas, police department and I recently got together here. Smitty helped me rebuild a billboard. We worked hard and had a great reunion. Our great fear was that some of

our old troopers would drive by and see two ole retired captains doing real, honest-to-goodness work. We weren't sure they could handle that. Luckily, there were no fatal crashes on the highway we worked adjacent to, so I guess we skated on that concern.

On a larger scale, I've attended reunions of my police cadet class from back in the 1970s. Nearly all of the 35 other police officers from that class have now retired, at least those who stayed for a career. Sadly, some are not still alive. When we get together, we tell some pretty tall tales. We all seem to have gotten shorter and wider. Must be those donuts.

It's possible, though, that I recently attended the most unusual reunion I'll ever experience. Until, of course, I go next time. During 2006, I was closely associated with a security group for 10 months. One of the most secure security groups that exist. Maximum security inmates from New Mexico's maximum security prison in Santa Fe. I spent almost a year as a fellow prisoner with them as a result of my involvement in a police shooting here in December 2004.

"You're nuts," said some of my cop friends, when I mentioned that my maximum security inmate friends were having a reunion at a city park in Albuquerque on August 30, 2009; had invited me; and I planned to go. "Since when," I responded, "have I let a little mental imbalance stop me from doing something that seemed like the right thing to do?"

7

A Good Man Who
Lived on a Small Hill

October 2009

Jim Madron died August 31, 2009. He wasn't quite 62. This isn't an obituary, just a final salute to an ole Vietnam War Marine Corps veteran who deserves one.

For several years Jimmy lived on a small hill in a small trailer overlooking Mayhill. He was a good man, a good citizen, who would call the sheriff's office when he saw anything out of order. He operated a car repair business in two different Mayhill locations. He was an honest man, a nice man.

I frequently saw Jim at Cloudcroft High School athletic events. He wasn't a yeller or a screamer but was there in a quiet way to support a stepson.

In later years he lived in Alamogordo. His health was not good and he had to leave the mountain. With son Billy, he operated the mail contract service between Mayhill, Cloudcroft and Alamogordo. I last saw

Jim about two months ago. Very ill, he still had a smile on his face, a positive spirit. He was always a friend.

A large crowd attended Jim's funeral in Hope, NM, that wide spot in the road we pass through on our way to Artesia. The little cemetery is about two miles south of the village, tough to find. The large size of the crowd attested to the kind of man Jim Madron was. He lies next to his parents, who both died in 1951.

A young Marine presented the U. S. flag to Jim's grandson, Travis. Jim Madron lives on the Big Hill now, overlooking all of us. Thanks, Jim, for your brave service, for being who you were. Rest in peace.

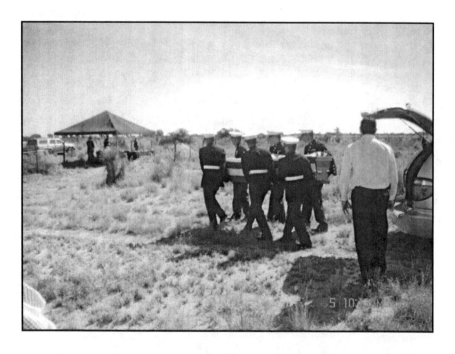

In 2009, six young US Marines carry Jim Madron
to his final resting place near Hope, New Mexico.

8

Thanksgiving Is For the Birds

November 2009

On four occasions lately, I've had near misses with turkeys – big birds - flying across Highway 82 between Cloudcroft and Mayhill. Guess they know what's coming and they're running for it.

Flying turkeys are like rocks with feathers. They'll put a sizeable bird bump in your car, or worse yet, cause you to lose control. If you see one, watch for more. They travel in bird herds.

I like birds, though. I've had two parrots, Richard and Herman, for pets. We won't count Lucy. We'd just gotten her when my son, thinking she couldn't fly, took her outside. Lucy was last seen headed towards the Pacific Northwest from Texas. I suspect something, a hawk perhaps, soon invited her over for lunch. Those green and red feathers had to look pretty tasty.

A policeman friend, Walter, gave us a duck since we lived at a lake. Naturally, we called the duck Walter. It was an Easter duck, had been raised in a kiddie wading pool. At first, Walter – the duck, not the policeman – wouldn't stay in the lake. He didn't like tadpoles nibbling on

his feet. Walter was a green-headed duck and was a lover, not a fighter. There were no other green-headed ducks on our lake when Walter arrived but soon there were many. He had quickly adjusted to tadpoles, and obviously to girl ducks.

We had three pet geese at the lake. Nigel – the mother – and Junior and Bella LaGoosey. They were great pets, very friendly. Unless the neighbor's grandsons were chasing them. Then they chased back.

I've tired of the rat race, since the rats so often win. Anyway, like what you've done or are doing, I put 50 years of life ingredients into Work Stew and think it's time for a little dessert. So this year has been one of travel. As a student of Civil War history, there were a couple of places I'd long wanted to visit.

One is Ft. Jefferson, on the Dry Tortugas 70 miles west of Key West, Florida. Yep, way out in the Gulf of Mexico. This fort was built to protect 1800s shipping, sort of a Gibraltar of the Gulf. Have you heard the saying, "Your name is mud"? Dr. Samuel Mudd, who treated John Wilkes Booth's broken leg after Booth assassinated President Lincoln, was sentenced to life imprisonment, did his time at Ft. Jefferson. He was pardoned after four years, having worked hard to help Federal soldiers survive smallpox.

The other is Ft. Sumter where the first shot of the Civil War was fired, at Charleston, South Carolina. I got to both places this summer.

Wait. Didn't I start off talking about birds? Hey, you're paying attention. En route to those Civil War forts, I had interesting encounters with birds.

Headed for Ft. Jefferson through a small central Florida town, I pulled into the Angry Apple Diner for lunch. Something on the car parked next to mine caught my eye. What tha'…? There was a very large bird sitting on top of that car, facing the restaurant's window. Was it a pet,

attached there with a leg chain, waiting on its owner? Was it a toy, a stuffed bird? It stood very still. I walked over, looked pretty closely but stayed out of beak range, just in case. It turned its head slowly, stared me down.

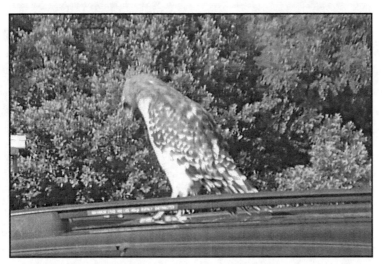

Henry the Hawk ready for lunch outside the Angry Apple Diner in Dunnellon, Florida.

About 18 inches tall, it looked at me as if to say: "My human friend, those are delicious looking eyeballs. May I have them? Bring them closer, please."

It seemed to be a hawk, and it seemed real enough. I backed off, went inside. "Do you know there's a very large bird on top of a car, right there, outside your window?" I asked the cashier. She was Lisa, the owner. "Oh, sure. That's Henry. He's just hungry. Actually he's always hungry. He's a bottomless pit. He lands on the car closest to that window and squawks when he wants to eat."

Well, okay then. It was just Henry. I asked for more of the story. Lisa explained that Henry the Red Shouldered Hawk has been around the Angry Apple for about 15 years now. She – Lisa – has looked after

him for the past seven. They feed him chicken entrails. (Henry, how disgusting is that?) At the back door, there's a steel post, a parking protector. The chicken meat is placed on that post. Henry swoops down and gets it.

Lisa lives seven miles away. Henry knows her car, follows her home. On her arrival, he's sitting in a nearby tree. Lisa only feeds Henry at the café. At one time she'd feed him by hand, hold up some chicken, but then her hand and Henry's talon became entangled. Lisa – after a few stitches - no longer does that. Henry is very cute but isn't the most popular bird in town. Every now and then he eats someone's kitten or baby duck, live chicken, whatever. Lisa preferred I didn't send her hometown newspaper a copy of this story. Oh, Henry eats snakes, though, not a bad thing.

Once Henry was acting strange while perched over some bushes near the restaurant. Lisa found a five foot alligator hidden there. Way to go, Henry! "May I see Henry eat?" I asked. Lisa put some chicken on the post. Henry wasn't in sight. Soon, though, he swooped down, taloned up the chicken, brushed my shoulder with his wing tip as he left. So cool. And I still had my eyeballs, thank you Lord. And so long, Henry.

In Charleston, headed to Ft. Sumter, I ducked into a Waffle House for breakfast. Or tried to. Four ducks – a mother and her three teenaged children - were blocking the door. Yes, on the sidewalk, blocking, and they didn't want to move. Finally gaining entrance, I asked the ladies inside: "Are those your ducks?" "Yes, they're our ducks. We feed them. They live in the pond across the parking lot." Mary, the manager, explained that there had been five ducks, but something - maybe a hawk – got one when it was little. (I kept quiet about Henry.) Rochelle, Mary and Nikki came outside with me and fed the ducks some bread. It looked good. Inside, I asked: "'Got any more of that bread? I'll take some French toast."

What does all this mean? I'm not sure, but I do appreciate birds as part of the great world we live in. I hope you have a big tasty one on your Thanksgiving Day table, one that won't peck your eyes out or eat your bread. I hope the Good Lord has blessed you as much as He's blessed me. I hope you understand how much I appreciate you, the people of Cloudcroft, New Mexico, and vicinity. Happy Thanksgiving!

9

Keeping Our Promises To A True Man of the West

December 2009

Cooperstown, New York, is more than 2,000 miles from Cloudcroft. It's probably best known as the location of the National Baseball Hall of Fame. Do you know anyone from there? A man named William Cooper settled the place. I bet you're acquainted with at least two of the town's natives. One of them was William Cooper's son.

The son, James Fennimore Cooper, is one of our more famous American authors. His best known work is "The Last of the Mohicans". Cooperstown is on the southern tip of Lake Otsego, in the foothills of the Catskill Mountains. Cooper referred to Lake Otsego in his writings as "The Glimmerglass", because of its peaceful, serene beauty. At its southern end, at Cooperstown, Lake Otsego gives birth to the Susquehanna River. The Susquehanna flows more than 400 miles, emptying into Chesapeake Bay in Maryland.

Cooperstown is bigger than Cloudcroft. I know it's larger because it has a stoplight. One. I'm glad we have one less. I'm not fond of stoplights.

Canadian poet Robert Service was quoted as saying: "A promise made is a debt unpaid." Almost five years ago I promised to visit the Cooperstown, New York, area. I paid that debt this past September.

When we think of New York, we usually think of the millions of people in New York City. But the majority of the state is mostly rural with mountains, dairies, timber, rivers, lakes. Gorgeous country. Green country.

The other Cooperstown person you're familiar with left that beautiful area behind to settle in New Mexico. I think he'd become enchanted with our state. Hey, we're not called the Land of Enchantment for nothing.

You see, the other person was Deputy Sheriff Robert Hedman, Jr., born in Cooperstown on July 2, 1955. Yes, Bob Hedman, who gave his life for you, the citizens of Otero County, New Mexico, on December 18, 2004. Five years ago. At his funeral, I promised his mother I'd come see her and Bob's brothers, his other family and friends.

After all, I was the last person who talked to Bob on this good earth. It was important for closure that I go. For them. For me, too. And, I wanted to know more about this man, my friend. Why did he really stay in New Mexico? What was he all about? What are his family and friends like? Why was he a cowboy, why did he like horses so much? I wanted to see his birthplace, his homes, his school.

Bob completed a career in the Army at White Sands Missile Range with 21 years service in 1994. He remained in New Mexico after military service because New York state taxes are so high. But to leave family and friends so far behind, it had to be more than that.

En route to New York, I drove into Washington, DC, to the National Police Memorial. I traced Bob's name on the wall with my finger. It was an honor to be there. I was touched by the presence of a distraught young woman about 20 years of age. I tried to console her. Her mother, a Los Angeles police officer, was killed in a train crash in that city last year. The memorial is a serious place.

I stayed in the Cooperstown area about four days, seeing Bob's old haunts. As a baby, he lived at Cobb's Knobb, The Glimmerglass in the near distance. By the age of three months, he traveled with his mother in a horse-drawn sleigh as they delivered milk. The old home site is gone, only the corn silo remains. With my propensity to give everyone a nickname, Bob Hedman was lucky I didn't know of that place. Bob of Cobb's Knobb would have been hard to resist! Perhaps riding in that sleigh guaranteed his future love of horses.

Knowing that the apple doesn't normally fall far from the tree, I asked about Bob's father. His dad had polio, his right side was paralyzed, but he refused to accept disability, always worked. When Bob was 16, a neighbor suggested that Bob's father take a disability benefit. Bob's reply on behalf of his father: 'Mind your own business!"

Bob's brothers told me their dad always said there were two important "R's" in life and they were Respect and Responsibility, not Rest and Relaxation. Bob learned that lesson well.

We visited Crumhorn Mountain Lake where Bob was a Boy Scout, attaining Scouting's second highest award. He first visited New Mexico at age 15 when he attended the premier high altitude Scout camp, Philmont, near Cimarron. His work on the Eagle award - Scouting's highest achievement - was cut short by his enlistment in the Army at age 18.

(During his work as a deputy in Otero County, Bob once rescued a wounded eagle. His former Scoutmaster, knowing of that and learning of Bob's death here in 2004, carved an eagle on a pedestal and presented it to Bob's mother. It's now a fixture at the corner of her home.)

Bob's brothers showed me the woods where they hunted coons, using Bob's favorite Blue Tick Hound, "Henry". It was a great way to earn money. They were paid $30 a pelt, big money in those days.

In the township of Schenevus, Bob's mother and I ate at the Big Chief Restaurant. It's named for Chief Schenevus, a strong chief of the Speckled Trout, of the Iroquois nation. One legend of the Speckled Trout goes like this: Chief Schenevus' favorite was a daughter, Manaho, who loved Manatee. Manaho, seeing her and Manatee's reflection in a favorite pool, told him: "We'll always be together." A jealous competitor for Manaho's attentions pushed Manatee to his death, into that same pool. Then Manaho drowned herself there, fulfilling her promise to always be with Manatee.

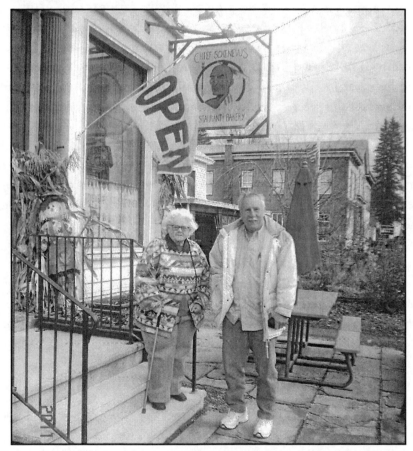

Deputy Bob Hedman's mother and I visit the Big Chief Restaurant in Schenevus, New York during 2011.

We visited Schenevus Central School where Bob graduated from high school. He grew up with legends such as that of Chief Schenevus. Probably another reason he felt comfortable in New Mexico, with our large population of Native American peoples.

I saw, I asked, I listened. I was beginning to know the family better, to know Bob Hedman better. But I was still a bit unsure as to why Bob Hedman choose to remain in New Mexico. His home is a beautiful place, and he was obviously a family oriented person. I attended a barbeque at the Oneonta, New York, Moose Club. About 35 of Bob's family and close friends were present. Conversations were many and varied. A sister-in-law of Bob's – he was a cowboy at heart – remarked that he was always fascinated with Western history like that of Lincoln County. Bob had worked as a deputy for Lincoln County at one time and his sister-in-law told me his deputy's commission there was probably his favorite piece of police memorabilia. The stories of Sheriff Pat Garrett, Billy the Kid, and others really lit him up.

Even now, and in view of Bob's death, one of his brothers talks of moving here. His sister-in-law remarked – off the cuff- that during a visit here once she felt a strange attraction to New Mexico. Her exact comment: "I felt I was meant to be in the West."

I think that's it, then. Bob Hedman was from the Northeast. From a beautiful place. But perhaps from his first trip here at age 15…from his military service here at White Sands Missile Range…from his cowboy ways and fascination with Western history…like his sister-in-law, Bob Hedman felt he was meant to be in the West. And here he was.

10

The Year of the Boat

January 2010

Another New Year upon us! Wow, how these years zip along. Are you doing something to make yours memorable? I find that if I don't take positive action to note a year in my memory, it may note itself through my inaction.

Hey, let's do something crazy this year so that we might remember it! Okay?

Think back. Why do you remember such and such a year? One of my favorites is 1996. The Year of the Atomic Move. Deciding early in 1996 - about May - to move to Cloudcroft, I was involved in all the planning such a move dictates. Leaving a job - selling a house - notifying the relieved relatives - etc.

In the midst of all that, in July 1996 I joined my oldest son - then a Navy fighter pilot - in a five day trip across the Pacific Ocean - Pearl Harbor, Hawaii, to San Diego. We were on the nuclear-powered aircraft carrier, the USS Nimitz. Later that fall, Thanksgiving Day to be exact, I drove into Cloudcroft.

Combining the two events, thus - 1996, the Year of the Atomic Move. A year I won't forget.

Some years just name themselves if we don't. Like 2008, for example. My mother and stepfather died, within 50 days, in mid-year. Earlier that year, I spent much time in Louisiana while they were ill. Afterwards, I spent more time in Louisiana remodeling their home, then selling it.

While there, I met a woman named Rita. Up close and personal. Too bad she was a hurricane. Rita seriously rained on my 2008 parade. It was The Year of the Raging Cajun, and I was the Cajun.

The events of 2008 dictated many of the terms of 2009. The Year of the Cleanup. While acting as executor of my mother's estate, I saw the value of cleaning up my own act. So during 2009 I worked hard to organize my shop - get rid of unnecessary projects - even sort out my photo albums. I'm not there yet but have progressed. Whew. Hard work.

Last month I wrote about a trip to New York during 2009. So my work was balanced by seeing Bob Hedman's hometown, Cooperstown, New York - the Baseball Hall of Fame - Niagara Falls - Gettysburg, PA - Ft. Sumter, SC - Kitty Hawk, NC - Ft. Jefferson, FL. Therefore 2009 was also the Year of the Low Budget Traveler, for me. Not bad on balance.

Way back now to 1987, the Year of the Unfinished Boat Trip. A friend and I attempted to break the Guinness Book Record for canoeing the length of the Mississippi River. Twenty three days, 10 hours, 20 minutes to do 2,510 miles. For various reasons, our attempt failed. Thus 1987 left a lingering unfinished taste in my mouth. So, hello, 2010.

Hopefully I'm now smarter, wiser, more sensible than to want to paddle that distance. Oh, also older. Thus I'm headed to St. Paul, MN, in the spring, to travel by boat to New Orleans, more than 2,000 miles. A powerboat, with only an emergency paddle.

Hold on a minute, there. Don't be picturing a Mississippi Queen riverboat. Think instead 1962 Lone Star El Dorado, the smallest cabin cruiser that Lone Star Boats, formerly of Grand Prairie, TX, ever made. Just 18 feet long, powered by about a 50HP outboard. Refurbishing the boat for the trip is my winter project. Underway as we speak.

Very basic but basically luxury compared to a canoe. For one thing, it has a roof. Do you know how much we take a roof for granted? How handy they are during such happenings as thunderstorms, hail? During the 1987 attempt, we met hail up close and personal in the Minnesota backwoods - on a wild rice lake. Trees offer no realistic haven, too many cows have found about that when lightning struck.

The paddle blade - held over the head - offered the only immediate protection. Beaching the canoe and crawling underneath - what we did second - was the only realistic alternative. Hail hurts.

I actually have two Lone Star El Dorados - a 1961 and a 1962. They're being combined into one, then I'll sell the leftover parts. Luxury? Total investment thus far is just over a thousand bucks, for the two boats - two trailers - one motor. They're old and cheap. But the result will have a roof, a small cabin that one can sleep full length in, eat in when necessary. Camping on the water. A smaller real life Gilligan's Island Minnow.

The most danger? Tugboats pushing a 40 to 60 string of barges, too powerful, too unwieldy to get out of your way. Powering upriver, throwing up a wake six feet or more tall. So your outboard and your small backup engine have to be in great condition. Make darn sure you stay out of their way.

Someone suggested I name the boat Billygan's Island. I'll pass on that, but Cloudcroft, New Mexico, will be prominently displayed on the side. Promoting a visit to the land of the waters of the Rio Penasco and Grindstone Lake will be undertaken at every opportunity.

Add to this a trip to the General Clinton Regatta, a 70 mile flatwater canoe race, in Cooperstown during Memorial Day - I promised Bob's mother I'd come back - and there it is. 2010, the Year of the Boat. Even if 2010 sends something else along, I've got some counterbalance.

Yes…if I can just get my plans in sync with whatever the Good Lord has in mind, we'll make it. So far He's been very good to me.

What will YOU do to make 2010 a Year to Remember? Maybe such plans as the above are too physically demanding, too time consuming if you're working. But you can make it - The Year of the Family Vacation - The Year of the Photo Album, the Autobiography - The Year I Got Back in Touch with the Grandson - etc.

I challenge you to make 2010 your own Year of the Boat - whatever kind of boat you choose to float in. Let's take a ride we won't forget!

Author's note, 2015: My oldest son and I did paddle and complete the General Clinton Canoe Regatta in Cooperstown, NY, during May 2010. Chapter 15 has that story. The Mississippi River boat trip, though, remains on the bucket list as it was put aside for a sailboat crossing of the Gulf of Mexico during 2010. See Chapters 20 and 21.

11

I Hate Wintertime in Cloudcroft

February 2010

February and we're smack in the middle of winter. I don't like the cold and snow. Can't do anything. Brrrrr. Keeps me indoors too much.

Well…there are one or two things I guess I like okay. I like talking to Helen and Barry and Gina and Dan at the Aspen's Cross Eyed Moose Café. I like drinking coffee there when the snow is falling. I like remembering good times there too with Doug, Brenda, Carlos and Vickie, in past years.

Oh, and I like going to the Western on a real cold day, having a Wayland Special and asking Liz about Bobby. I like the pancake that comes with the Wayland. About the size of the hubcaps I used to have on my '55 Ford. And the pancake likes my stomach, about the size of the trunk I used to have on my '55 Ford.

Okay, I like dropping into Big Daddy's every now and then for my favorite meal there, the hot shrimp basket. Makes me feel like I'm on the Texas coast, on a cold day. I wonder if they fly those shrimp in fresh daily?

Cafes like the Cross Eyed Moose beckon on cold winter days, shown here in 2010.

Yes, I'll admit it…I like going to the Texas Pit on a cold day, eating those hot pork ribs…asking Heather about her mom. "How's your mom doing in Alabama?" I'll ask. "Oh, she's doing fine," she'll answer. Seems to be the right kind of question and answer session we'd have during the winter, nothing too complicated.

It must be that I like going to restaurants in the wintertime. Because I also like eating a cheeseburger at Chuck's place, asking Judy: "How 'bout them Cowboys?" I especially like asking Judy that question this winter since Chuck's Steelers didn't make the playoffs. Oh, that's cold, isn't it? A good wintertime jab.

Hmmm. I just remembered it's fun to go to the Front Porch on a cold day, say hello to Abbie and the others. And to the Mayhill Café, good food, good people! Warms me up on a cold winter day just to think about it.

Cold winter days with snow on the ground keep me from hiking in the forest. Well…sometimes when the snow isn't too heavy, I do like to go out to the Silver-Saddle-Apache campground, walk that trail down by the rock pit. During a gentle snowfall, it's so peaceful and quiet, I can hear the snow hitting the ground. And my hearing isn't perfect. Maybe it's making a thumping sound I don't notice. Anyway, what I hear is a pleasing thing.

Wintertime gives me an opportunity to work on writing projects, since the cold weather makes it nice to stay inside and stay warm. So I get things done I otherwise might not.

Oh, I like going to my shop and firing up the big wood heater which keeps my working space about 50 degrees even on the worst days. Out of the weather and warm enough to get things done, like an engine swap on my old Scout that Doug Huntsucker helped me with. We got something accomplished and had fun too, still talk about it.

It's a great time to go to the Post Office at 10 AM and meet with friends, catch up on what's happening while our feet drip melted snow onto the floor. A great way to burn daylight!

The Cloudcroft library beckons on cold days, good chance to visit with Joyce and pick up a new book.

Come to think of it, do I really hate winter? Isn't one of the reasons I love living here because of the change of seasons? Think I'll go inside now, stoke up the wood heater, prop my feet up and think about this while I have a relaxing cup of hot chocolate.

One cannot make hasty decisions on a cold February day. Time to contemplate…

12

The Little Black Trailer – Saving Money in a Tough Economy

March 2010

Cloudcroft, of course, has been affected by hard economic times. Like you, I try to be careful with limited resources.

Recently, needing a small utility trailer, I shopped and found one that was suitable for $300, but felt that pricewise I could do better. Diligently, I continued my search.

I have a garden tiller I inherited. It has a small 5 HP Briggs & Stratton engine. But it would take a Caterpillar Gargantua El Destructo model – the kind used in old Japanese monster movies – to till the rocks in my yard. So I wondered, could I trade the tiller for a utility trailer? I don't want to garden anyway. After a couple of potential trades fell thru, though, I decided I'd just buy a trailer. (Most everyone here has those same rocks.)

Locating better deals on a trailer for $275, then $250, then $225, I was getting closer. Then I found one for $200. Almost there, but I was certain I could use my handyman skills to buy something needing

just a little fixing, and save even more. The perfect deal was out there somewhere.

Suddenly, eureka! An Internet ad, on the Craig's List website, had just the wording I was looking for. I knew, here was my trailer! I could get this rascal for almost nothing. Except for the phone number, the ad appeared exactly as follows: (Read and sense the desperation of the seller, as I did.)

MUST SELL!!!! MOVING AND MUST SELL BY 1/20/2010. 40 INCH BY 8 FOOT HOMEMADE TRAILER. NEEDS SOME WORK. PLEASE MAKE OFFER. CALL 575-555-5555.

An accompanying photo showed a tiny, rusting, forlorn little trailer, one end of a 2X4 siding piece sitting on the ground. The whole thing looked sad, lonely, neglected, forgotten. A perfect candidate for membership in the Billy Fleet!

And – wow! Words like MUST SELL and PLEASE make my day. NEEDS SOME WORK? Heck, everything needs SOME work, not to worry. And it was only 50 miles away, just a 100 mile roundtrip. Surely we all know how reasonable gasoline is now.

So naturally, I called. It was even better than I thought. Shawn had lost his job, had to vacate his house in two days, have everything out of the landlord's yard. Hey, I was convinced this little trailer could be had for ten or twenty bucks! "I'm on my way!" I exclaimed, without agreeing on a price. I got directions, drove the 50 miles.

In his back yard, Shawn and I looked at the trailer. The photo hadn't done it justice. In person, it looked worse. "Are the wheel bearings good?" I asked. "Does it have wheel bearings?" Shawn asked back.

We went inside to do the final haggling and the paperwork. I prepared to move in for the kill, ready to spring.

Woe is me. Enter Kayla, 4, and Morgan, 3, from down the hall. Two cute little girls. Rivet the Labrador retriever barked from his kennel. Rivet sounded a little weak, like he needed a doggie treat. The place was a shambles, a desperate move was in progress.

Kayla looked up at me, remarked with friendly four year old logic: "Hi. You're a big guy like our daddy." Why, yes, little girl, I am, and don't try to schmooze me, I'm here to rip off your trailer. So what if you've played in it with your Barbie? I thought. But I felt the first tremor of hesitation, the first weakening. (Wife/mother sat quietly in the living room, holding another little one in diapers.)

A little less certain, I tried to continue. "What's your rock bottom, Shawn?" I asked. I love that term, rock bottom. I learned it from a Cloudcroft hustler friend of mine who was trying to get his mother's wedding ring from her, to pawn.

"Well…I think it should be worth at least $50," he replied, "for the parts if nothing else." I glanced at Kayla and Morgan, at Rivet. "Sounds good to me," I caved, thanking the Good Lord Shawn hadn't said he thought it was worth $200 or more. I dug out the money, as Kayla and Morgan continued talking to me. Kid talk, cute talk.

Good grief. I remembered a ten spot that two Senior Center ladies and I saw simultaneously on the Allsup's parking lot once, a bill I beat them to like a New Orleans Saint on a Dallas Cowboy loose football. I gave Shawn the $10 as well. "Buy Kayla and Morgan some ice cream at the Dairy Queen, will you? And get Rivet a dog bone if there's anything left over," I said.

Well, heck, Shawn had lost his job, and $50 for a trailer wasn't bad anyway. (No, you cannot count the extra ten bucks, that was for ice cream and a dog biscuit.) I could still save a lot of money by fixing up this little rusty trailer.

Over the next few days…let the savings begin. And DO NOT count the three days labor, either. What do I have but time?

Lowe's - lumber/hardware/paint/paint brushes, $98.78. Harbor Freight - tongue jack and taillights, $52.89. Kmart - spray paint, $8.46. Back to Lowe's - drill bits, painter's tape, pop rivets, another $33.34. Walmart - forgot the spray primer paint, $5.05. And those wheel bearings? A bit noisy. Northern Equipment - $32.78…plus the wheel bearing grease at AutoZone - $6.15. Oops, forgot some wiring for the taillights, back to Harbor Freight - for the final $19.06.

Let's see? How much did I save? Out with the calculator here. Hmmm? Counting the $50 purchase price, my total cost was $306.51. And the weather cracked tires I'll have to replace not too far down the road? Hold on, now, don't get sassy with me. That'll be routine maintenance which - like the ice cream money, the doggie treat and the labor - cannot legally be included.

I hope each of you has learned a valuable lesson from my experience about how to save money during these troubled times. (I've only understood in recent years that my college economics professor was just kidding when he said: Buy high, sell low.)

Anyway, may God bless your efforts to make wise use of your assets. And if you save so much that you need a small trailer to haul your cash to the bank, I know where you can rent one very reasonably.

If a tire blows out, though, you've gotta replace it. Just routine maintenance, not part of the rental fee, you understand.

13

Moondog Moretti, Trains, Neil Mitchell, and Other Things

April 2010

Trains on the brain.

Maybe it's the aura of the Cloud Climbing Railroad that still lingers here in the Sacramentos. But today I think how incredibly lucky we are to make at least part of our trip on the Life Journey Express that runs through Cloudcroft.

There's a sense of community here that although perhaps equaled elsewhere, is not exceeded. Let me explain.

Chasing down a boat part elsewhere recently, I found myself checking into a Mobile, Alabama, motel about midnight. Large numbers of very large men were in the lobby, outside room doors, all about.

What's happening? I wondered aloud. "Retired pro wrestler's convention," was the desk clerk's answer.

Well. I've never spoken to a pro wrestler before, only have yelled at a couple of them from a safe distance.

I eased quietly into my room, between two groups of wrestlers. Wouldn't want to upset my neighbors, would I? Course not. I was wired, though, from 13 hours of driving, so took in my March issue of The Mountain Monthly. I wanted to go to sleep with thoughts of Cloudcroft, not something extreme from USA Today.

R. L. Posey's letter about Neil Mitchell caught my eye. I have absence ignorance, having dodged much snow, ice and cold weather this winter in pursuit of boat restoration in a warmer clime. Neil sick? I remember meeting him the first time in 1998.

Then, Neil was grading roads in an isolated place, near Telephone Canyon, off Aqua Chiquita Canyon, near Sacramento. He couldn't be reached by phone. His family was concerned. I was a new deputy, and it was part of my job to deliver emergency messages. Neil was fine. We chatted for a few minutes, but he excused himself pretty quickly.

"Sorry, gotta go. Gotta make a living," he said. Hey, no problem. Self-employed people are my heroes anyway in this world we live in. It takes guts that many of us don't have.

Trains on the brain persist…

I don't know how the Mitchells came to be in the Cloudcroft area, but I do know that Neil might have a different wife but for a long ago train trip. Cressie wouldn't be here.

Ever hear of the Orphan Trains?

Here's a quote from the National Orphan Train Complex, Inc., of Concordia, Kansas:

"Between 1854 and 1929 an estimated 200,000 orphaned, abandoned,

and homeless children were placed out during, what is known today, as the Orphan Train Movement…

When the Orphan Train movement began, it was estimated that 30,000 abandoned children were living on the streets of New York City…aid institutions developed a program that placed homeless children into homes throughout the country. The children were transported to their new homes on trains which were eventually labeled "Orphan Trains."

Cressie's grandfather – a tiny three year old New York City street urchin - was on one of those trains, wound up in the Pecos River Valley with only his eight year old sister. Alone. Together.

Ever heard of the term, "Put Up For Adoption"? Like others, on arrival Cressie's grandfather and great aunt were put up on the train platform. Local citizens inspected them for their general health, the soundness of their teeth. I guess their teeth were good because they were taken, grew up out West, although in different nearby homes.

I went to sleep that night thinking that Neil couldn't be in a better place to deal with sickness. We passengers on the Cloudcroft Cannonball might be a little short of ticket money when the conductor comes through – we might misplace our luggage – Jesse James might have robbed the train, taken our Timex - but our fellow riders will get us through the trip. I know. Though not for an illness, I've taken that ride. I also know you'll help Neil and Cressie.

Next morning…leaving the motel…large numbers of pro wrestlers still standing around. Don't these guys sleep? I thought. I sensed a story, even though I realized I might have to tell it from the top of a nearby tree.

I approached a group of four.

"Hey guys, ever hear of Cloudcroft, New Mexico? I write stories for the newspaper there. Got a minute?" "Sure," they replied, at least in body language.

Moondog Ed Moretti of Hidden Valley Lake, California, held the rope up, let me into the ring. Bobby Simmons and Scrappy McGowan of McDonna, Georgia, hit me with the High and Low. Martin Rigsby of Eclectic, Alabama, rearranged my arms so they both hung on the right side of my body. "Better for taking notes," he explained. Then Moondog introduced me to the Pile Driver. And I don't mean the kind of piles us older guys are more familiar with. Ouch!

Moondog looks like a good guy to have on your side in a bar fight. Anyway, I'm always respectful to very large men who wear studded collars.

Moondog Moretti, ready to rumble!

It was time to leave. But I had one dumb question left. "Martin, do you hate cops?" I asked. Martin, who still wrestles and is 6'6", weighs 279, replied: "Man, I love cops. They've escorted me out of some of the nastiest places, in one piece." Well, of course. Thank God, love conquers all.

14

Hey Ma! Thinking of You...Hope You're Still Dancin'!

May 2010

"There's a church in the valley in the wildwood
No lovelier place in the dell
No spot is so dear to my childhood
As the little brown church in the dell"

Many of you recognize the words from the old song, Church in the Wildwood. James Canyon Church, with its small, quiet cemetery, is such a place. As a community, we've visited there often lately. Too often, it seems.

Sometime before May 9th, I'll visit a similar spot - be it a little flatter - in rural Mississippi. It'll be a Mother's Day visit. This will be my second such occasion without my mother, and I miss her.

The little country church where she's buried is dear to my childhood. My great-grandparents donated the land, and as a youngster I was a frequent visitor. At her grave site, I'll focus on the good times we had.

My mother was adventuresome and fun, a bit zany. Here's one esca-
pade I'll always remember. Inadvertently, it determined a significant
portion of my future, and my children's futures as well.

She took my sister and me on our first airplane ride. Oh...it was her
first plane ride, too. My dad worked in Central America - Honduras -
in the 1950s. We planned to spend the summer of 1953 with my father
in the small village of Guaimaca. He had a lumber camp there, about
80 kilometers northeast of Honduras' capital, Tegucigalpa.

We obtained passports in New Orleans, returned later to travel to
Honduras on TACA Airlines, still in operation today. Laying on a mo-
tel room bed the night before our flight, we studied Spanish. I was a
nervous and excited 10 year old who didn't sleep too well.

My dad wanted my mother to bring his German Luger pistol. "How
can I get it through customs?" she asked. "With a couple of cartons
of Camels," he replied, "no problem." Mordida - the bribe, the little
bite - was an established practice. She carried the gun in a big purse,
underneath the cigarettes.

I recall the aircraft being a Lockheed Constellation, a curvy sleek-look-
ing four engine propeller-driven craft. (I had no clue that 13 years later
I'd be flying across Vietnam to Taiwan on the same type of Air Force
plane when an engine would fail. The Connie, though, was sometimes
called the World's Finest Trimotor and returned us safely to Thailand. I
still didn't like the sight of that stationary prop out the window, or the
thought of guys named Charlie looking up, salivating.)

Back in 1953, our first stop was in Belize. No problem there. Next was
Guatemala City, Guatemala. Just our luck...we landed in the middle of
an attempt to overthrow the government. Herded into a room at the
airport, we were held for a couple of hours, couldn't leave. "Oh, well,"
I thought, "Mother has the Luger." Yeah, watch yourself, rebels, don't
mess with my ma.

The room had large windows that overlooked the runway. Guatemalan Air Force P-51 Mustangs - most likely U. S. WWII surplus fighter aircraft - were taking off with bombs attached, returning without them. Someone on the ground was having a whole lot more fun than we were. I was in the middle of a revolution, yet had complete confidence in my mother to keep me safe. Aren't mothers something?!

Finally allowed to leave, we arrived at our destination, Tegucigalpa. Only later in life did I learn it's one of the world's most dangerous airports. Surrounded by mountains, with a short runway, it requires very steep landings and takeoffs. But - what, me worry? - hey, my mom was there. With her Luger. And the cigarettes. We cleared customs as the inspector lit up the Camels.

What a fantastic summer! I hung out with native boys at the sawmill camp. Played with Richard, our parrot, and Chico, our monkey. (Monkeys are cute, aren't they?...but are very mischievous. Some things they do shouldn't be allowed. Like R-rated movies, no child under the age of 17 should be allowed to have one, unless his parents are present. The term "wild monkey" is still with me.)

We slept in hammocks. Visited banana plantations in our jeep, kept a stalk of fresh bananas hanging in the camp house. My mother used Pet condensed milk in cereal in place of fresh milk; made flapjacks that we ate with Karo syrup, the only kind available. We went to an occasional movie - with English sub-titles – in Tegucigalpa. Back then, the capital city had three neon signs.

Returning to the U. S., the flight was mostly routine. Guatemala was quiet. Over New Orleans, though, we encountered thunderstorms, circled the airport for more than an hour before finally landing safely. Hey, I was then the experienced air traveler, thanks to my mother's reassuring presence!

You know...it's just now occurred to me that my mother - on her first

plane ride too – with adult realization of the danger of being caught up in political turmoil, war - sneaking a gun through customs – flying near thunderstorms - was probably very frightened too...but maintained a calm demeanor for the sake of my sister and me.

That trip ignited my curiosity and interest in aircraft that persists to this day in our family. I became a commercial pilot, flew police helicopters. My sons were introduced to aviation in a small Cessna we had. My eldest became a Navy fighter pilot, is now an airline pilot. My middle son, born deaf, enjoyed parachuting. The youngest served as an Army helicopter Aero Scout.

At age seven, my daughter rode in her first helicopter. She carries my mother's first name as her middle name, incidentally. Iris. A beautiful flower.

My mother took her final flight on July 11, 2008, on the wings of angels. I was blessed to be holding her hand at the gate, as she boarded. If the Good Lord will let me repeat that routing someday, my mother will be at the other end, waiting. I just hope they made her check her Luger at the Pearly Gate, or she'll be shooting in the air.

Cowboys want to be buried with their boots on, right? Well, my mother wasn't a cowgirl, but she wanted to be buried with her red high-heeled shoes - her dancin' shoes - so she could "dance in heaven". Her early religious training frowned on dancing, but my mother was...well...my mother.

Just before her casket was sealed, I put those red shoes inside. My stepfather told me tearfully later that day...when they'd watch the Lawrence Welk show, my mother would say: "Close the blinds, Don. Dance with me." He died six weeks later, partly of illness, mostly of a broken heart. I hope they're still dancin'.

If your mom is still around, will you give her an extra hug on Mother's

Day? For those of us who've lost ours. We'll appreciate that, and I bet we'll feel a nice little squeeze the exact moment you do. Thanks, and Happy Mother's Day!

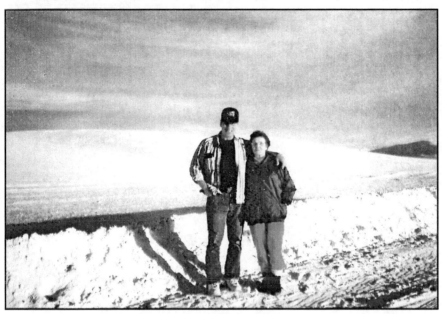

A 1996 visit to White Sands National Monument with my mother, Lucille Green.

15

Dam It! A Revolutionary Water Ride that Hurt So Good

July 2010

KA-BOOM!!!

KA-BOOM!!!

The ghost of Billy Mays selling a cleaning product? No way. It was two ear-splitting sonic booms caused by space shuttle Atlantis returning to Cape Canaveral, May 26, 2010. Overhead, Guido – Dominic Antonelli - my oldest son's former Navy squadron mate and the Atlantis' pilot, had the pedal to the metal, stirring up the heavens.

I had missed the launch but promised myself to be there for the landing if the Good Lord was willing and the creek didn't rise, at least not the Indian River at Cocoa Beach, Florida. And yes, I was standing on the river bank at 8:45 that morning, as Guido and the crew flashed by, then touched down safely. It was a real throat lumper!

Within 20 minutes, the New Mexico tag on my canoe trailer was following me up Interstate 95 towards Cooperstown, New York.

Deputy Sheriff Bob Hedman died near Cloudcroft on December 18, 2004. Last year I visited his family near Cooperstown. I promised to go back. The 48th annual General Clinton Canoe Regatta, held Memorial Day, was a great excuse. It's a 70 mile flatwater canoe race, the longest such one day event anywhere. It's a sport I've known before.

In 1779, Revolutionary War General James Clinton needed to move his army south to Tioga, New York. The Susquehanna River, its headwaters at the southern end of Lake Otsego at Cooperstown, was the logical mode of transportation, but the river was too shallow. So his men dammed the lake, hopped into boats...smashed the dam...and wooohoooo!...rode the flooded Susquehanna for miles.

This revolutionary water ride helped General Clinton's army quickly join other forces and defeat the British and Indians at the Battle of Newton, near today's Elmira, New York. Author James Fennimore Cooper described this "dammed" event - c'mon, that's a joke! - in his book, "The Pioneers".

The regatta begins with a 6 AM paddle a half mile out into Lake Otsego - called The Glimmerglass in Cooper's Leatherstocking Tales - around a moored boat...then back to the Susquehanna's beginning and over General Clinton's dam site.

My oldest son bravely volunteered to go along. As an 11 year old, he was to accompany me on a seven day Rio Grande trip, from Big Bend National park to Langtry, Texas. But he wisely broke his arm, couldn't go. Thus we've had a make-up trip pending for 31 years.

I've formerly done those distances, and more...But, the last time was 18 years ago. Never fear...we practiced...an hour and a half in Colorado this past April - sheeez. Well, mustn't overdo it so close to race time, right?

Folks, especially older folks, take my word for it...as if you already didn't know...the body changes a lot between 49 and 67...a whole lot!

I stay in pretty good shape, but sometimes the mind has an exaggerated notion of what its attached parts can reasonably do. Guilty on all counts!

So, 6 AM on May 31st found us paddling out onto the sure-enough glassy surface of The Glimmerglass. It was beautiful, and so historical. There were 242 other boats. It was cool at the start, but became the second hottest day on record in the 48 years of the race...humid, an 88 degree high.

Paddling onto Lake Otsego – The Glimmerglass – on Memorial Day, 2010.

We left the lake for the Susquehanna River, and shortly afterwards, made our first of three portages...over Cooperstown Dam, with Bassett Hospital about 100 yards to our right, where Bob Hedman was born. I felt his presence...

Northeasterners - and the many Canadians present - take their canoeing and kayaking very seriously. There was no chance we'd win anything...

our challenge, our goal, was simply to finish. (One of Bob's brothers, on learning we'd entered, remarked: "You're going to do WHAT?!? Are you SURE?" Ahhh, such confidence.)

Then...let the fun begin...paddling hour after hour...gravel bars...the heat...many moments of deep introspection...what the heck am I doing here?...can I really do this?...Bob's family - our bank team - faithfully meeting us with food and water...through Phoenix Mills...Hyde Park... Clintonville...Milford. Then Portlandville...the spirit of Bob Hedman in the boat, looking at me, smiling: "Billy, you gonna let the little ole Susquehanny beat you?"

Through three mile long Goodyear Lake, over the one-half mile portage at its dam, steep hills. Then by Colliersville...Emmons...Oneonta and over Oneonta Dam...will this ever end? We were the only team from out West, could we let you - New Mexico - down? No way!... then Otego...Wells Bridge...Always thinking, just 12 more minutes, one more mile...making a bit over five miles every hour...

Unadilla...Sidney...Riverside... Near the 55th mile, an adult American bald eagle made attack runs on the boat just ahead, the paddler in a bright red shirt, the eagle's talons coming close, protecting its nest? I had a bright red bandana around my neck, cringed as we passed within 30 feet, remembered that Native Americans believed the eagle a messenger from the heavens...

But c'mon!...Bob rescued an injured eagle once...Eagle Network, I mentally radioed, I'm a friend!... I wanted to hear "Roger that" - luckily the eagle just stared, never moved...

Finally - FINALLY - 13 hours, 10 minutes and 17 seconds from the start - General Clinton Park in Bainbridge, New York...oh sweet finish line, how lovely you looked! Bob's family got the boat out of the water. We were 208th overall of 216 boats that arrived, some taking almost 15 hours. Twenty-seven boats were apparently kidnapped by aliens.

The winning time? Just under eight hours by professionals from Michigan. They, not us, were the toughest guys in Otsego County, New York, that day. But race officials seemed to appreciate that we'd traveled so far and kindly gave my son and me the "Outstanding Effort" award, something we were grateful for.

That was Memorial Day, May 31, 2010, during which U. S. flags flew all along the 70 miles of river. Gatherings of families and friends in progress. While paddling I sometimes thought about the men and women who've put it all on the line so the rest of us can enjoy the American promise: Life, liberty and the pursuit of happiness.

My son and I were tired when we finished after 7 PM that night, but we were living life to the fullest, we were free and we were happy. Thank God for the privilege of being an American!

My "Outstanding Effort" trophy? I've mailed it back to New York State, to Bob Hedman's mother. No one ever gave more of an outstanding effort than her son.

16

When Tony the Tagger Tagged
the Tunnel of Love

August 2010

By now you've seen it. For about two months, someone has loved KLG. The obnoxious graffiti proclaiming that fact is painted on both sides of the westbound US Highway 82 tunnel entrance.

Those kinds of signs are embarrassing to a community and send the wrong message to visitors.

Who is KLG? Let's just call her Kute. For Kute Little Girl. She has to be cute, right?...for someone to risk life and limb climbing, crawling and clambering over rocks beside the tunnel.

Let's call the artist - although this isn't very artistic graffiti - Tony. Tony the Tagger, or TTT. I'm guessing the person is a young male, probably 9th through 11th grade. Why? A male because of the athleticism involved, and young because even high school seniors are too cool to engage in such juvenile-like behavior, and college students are way too cool. Besides, all the older kids have cell phones and are too

busy twittering, tweeting, Facebooking and YouTubing to paint on rocks.

Isn't writing on rocks basically an old-fashioned stone-age approach?

TTT isn't daring enough, of course, to sign his name. For the most part, taggers are cowards, aren't they? Everything done anonymously. They usually do their thing after midnight, about OhDark:30. Like rats.

Probably 1,000 people or more pass through the tunnel daily. A high traffic location. But I suspect there are precisely only four of those thousand who really care about Tony's feelings. TTT himself, KLG, DOG and MOG.

DOG and MOG would be Dad of Girl and Mother of Girl, nice folks probably worried silly about what their wantabe son-in-law will do next. Will he spray paint their house in a desperate attempt to woo their daughter?

Unfortunately, Tony's handiwork is like a Russian Thistle. In the Sacramentos, we know that plant. Allow it to bloom and spread its seed, and suddenly, it's everywhere. If Russian Thistle was a money crop, most of us James Canyoners would be rich.

Tony the Tagger should be identified, and at least have to clean up the mess he's made, and apologize to our community.

Ever been to Quito, Ecuador? Quito was recently named one of the Most Affordable places in the world. It's a quaint South American capital, at 9,000 feet elevation. U. S. citizens can live there comfortably on even $10 to $15 thousand a year.

Someone near and dear to me just returned from a visit to Ecuador - to Quito, the Andes and the Amazon rain forest. "What was your

impression, in a few words?" I asked. "Amazing," she responded, "but graffiti is everywhere in Quito, very ugly." What an embarrassing thing for Ecuador.

During my career with the San Antonio, Texas, police department, I headed a unit that tracked down graffiti artists. It was 1990 and we had more than 5,000 documented gangsters, each gang trying to outdo the other with its painted messages in public places. The problem was gigantic. Costs were astounding.

Aside from gang advertising, young men spray painted their messages of passionate love for their girlfriends. A popular Chicano phrase was "con safos". It was kind of a code of honor. If our TTT had spray painted his love for KLG in San Antonio, his graffiti would have been untouchable. Unalterable. If he'd marked it underneath with a "c/s". Con safos meant: You cannot disturb this.

A competitor for Kute's affection wasn't allowed, by the code, to touch or deface Tony's public declaration but had to paint his own, someplace else where it wouldn't detract from Tony's. "X-ing out" Tony's work wasn't allowed. The end result? Double graffiti.

We learned to thoroughly research and document the real cost of graffiti removal. This included: The initial assessment. Photos. Vehicle and labor costs. Color matching of the original paint surface. Paint removers, sandblasting, scrubbers, scrapers, paint brushes, new paint. What appeared to be a minor crime - a misdemeanor with less than $250 damage - could quickly add up to a felony amount.

Jail time wasn't as important as 160 hours of community service, helping remove those eyesores. It was astounding how four weeks of scrubbing and hard work curbed one's enthusiasm for spray painting signs in public places. Are you with me, Tony?

All of you, for years now and without knowing it, have looked at what

was a large expanse of graffiti just above the tunnel. A Tony-like sign had been painted on about a 5' X 3' rock. A natural billboard. Soon afterwards, I stopped and found a tiny rock that matched in color, took it to the paint store the next day.

About OhDark:30 that night, I returned and painted the entire rock, restoring it to a nice rock-like color. I felt good about my role in obscuring - to this day - that declaration of young love, but had some morning-after regret. You know the saying: "No good deed goes unpunished." How true. My good $75 Rocky police boots were covered with gray splatters and I had to replace them. And pay for the paint. Oh well.

Regarding the present graffiti, could Tony instead be Tonie? Could be. During 2000, nearly all the highway signs between Cloudcroft and Mayhill were tagged. But like a fine drop of Jack Daniels, a suspect's name soon filtered through the investigative charcoal. Yes, a young lady's name.

With her dad present, I interviewed - she denied - I wasn't convinced but was relieved. She was a good friend of my daughter's. Years later, my daughter told me…yes, her friend had been Tonie the Girl Tagger. She'd been very scared when questioned, and never repeated the act. Good enough.

As for Tony the current Tagger, what you've done is not GRREEEAAAAATTTTTTT!!! You've defaced the beautiful place we live, and you live here too. Like using your own bathroom and not flushing. Shame on you. But be careful if you go back to the tunnel. Perhaps God, with orders to Mother Nature, will be watching.

Consider this: A few years ago, I exited the tunnel, headed uphill, once again around OhDark:30, same place. And almost rear-ended a car fully stopped in the uphill lane. The car's left front door and trunk were open. The driver, a snake collector from Alamogordo, was on foot. I

watched as he caught, and placed into a burlap sack, a huge diamond-back rattlesnake. It was one of the largest I've ever seen.

That snake had just climbed, crawled and clambered out from the very rocks you, TTT, recently stood on to proclaim your undying love to KLG. That rattlesnake cured any clambering impulses for the area I've ever had. It would be tragic for you to get seriously hurt over something so silly.

About to enter the Highway 82 tunnel, westbound, May 2015, and it's graffiti free!

Be safe. Just mail her a card. An anonymous one if you're afraid her folks will find out who you are.

Or heck, sign your name and just write c/s underneath it. That way, they'll be honor bound to give her the card as is and can't write in the name of a prospective son-in-law they'd prefer.

17

Jane, May Your Future Travels Be On Happy Highways!

September 2010

Woe is me. After a five year relationship, Jane left me for another man.

During those years, we were enchanted in the Land of Enchantment. We visited the Kit Carson House at Taos. She was nearby while I fished at Red River. Close as I gazed at Wheeler Peak outside Angel Fire.

At Chama, we admired the Cumbres & Toltec Scenic Railroad. Saw fishermen snagging salmon at Navajo Lake near Aztec. She waited without complaint while I explored the Salmon Ruins near Farmington. Bravely took me across 30 miles of thunderstorm-threatened dirt road to Chaco Canyon.

We went to Jemez Springs, Los Alamos, Espanola. Later, I drove with Jane to Carlsbad Caverns, marveled at the wonders of nature there and at nearby Sitting Bull Falls.

But it wasn't all play. We tugged cars and boats to Albuquerque for

painting. She helped me tote construction materials, assisted my work trailer in following us.

But alas, Plain Jane, my 1993 GMC pickup, is no more. Not with me, anyway.

C'mon, folks, I'm not the only one who's formed an emotional attachment to a favorite ride. Many men have told me about their babies, their '55 Chevy, their '57 Ford. The ladies are guilty too. You've mentioned darting about in your Dodge Dart, valiantly driving your Plymouth Valiant. One woman's eyes smiled, remembering her Cricket. Cricket? Yep. Sold by Plymouth in the U. S. from 1971-73.

Some of my sweeties were a '49 Chevy, a '55 Ford Victoria, and 1955 and 1956 Chevy two-door hardtops.

I met Jane in Alamogordo in 2004. "Only 11,500 miles. Like new…" said the ad. Hmmm? A 12 year old car driven less than 1,000 miles per year? Had to see that. Opening the garage door, I was taken with her right away. Her smell was the essence of New Car #5 perfume. Jane, whose roommate was a classic Corvette, was a real babe.

The owner bought her new for a drag race truck. She was a short, regular cab model with a 350 V8 engine. A stick shift. Lots of horsepower. But His Ownership had never raced it, had hardly even driven it.

Jane was partially nude when we met. Got my attention. Many parts had been removed to reduce her weight. Not to get personal, but her tailgate was wrapped in plastic, in the attic. Her front bumper was in the kitchen. Numerous other parts were in boxes. Even her red GMC letters! How much can THEY weigh, I wondered?

She had roll-up windows, manual door locks, was born without an air conditioner. Plain Jane, then, had to be her name. Even so, she was lovely, but she had a serious issue.

You see, little Jane was a two wheel drive pickup. Small, light, 2WD, wrong for the mountain winters. I hesitated. But she had me from hello, and it was summertime. Winter snow was far away. When you want a thing... Thus, after the requisite haggling, a deal was struck.

Before I got her, though, the owner telephoned. "May I back out?" he asked. "I love this little truck and would really like to keep her." Well, who can mess with love? Not me. "Not a problem," I said. Bye, Jane, I thought. We could have made it, girlie.

A year later, same ad, same truck. Again I called. "Are you serious this time?" I inquired. "Yes, my teenage son is living here now. I'm not using the pickup, and if I don't sell it, he'll destroy it." I understood, and this time he wasn't kidding. So Jane moved to my place.

Wow, five great years! And yes, winter was a challenge. I carried weight in the bed. Usually firewood. We raced up snowy, icy hills. When the first snowflake of fall hit the windshield around High Rolls as we drove up the mountain, I'd say a little prayer. "Please, Lord, don't let the tires lose traction." A tow strap accompanied us, for our rescue, not to rescue others. Somehow, we always made it.

But the only permanent thing in life is change, isn't it? With retirement, I began to restore old boats. They've gotten larger, heavier. The latest, a 1957 Lone Star Starliner, is a 23 footer. Jane had the gumption but not the suspension for such work. And she wanted to discuss that. "We need to talk," she said.

Uh oh. The Talk. I've dodged those for years. But sometimes they're necessary. "Am I pulling them or are they pushing me? I'm not sure. If you're going to hang out with these giant water-borne hussies, these large mermaid-like hootchie mamas, you need a bigger truck, Billy Boy," she said. Sadly, by a lonely roadside where we'd stopped, I agreed.

Jane was still beautiful. Why not let her go? Enter the Internet, and

Jason. He found her on eBay. Or was it eHarmony? Once again, love at first sight!

We made the deal. Jason flew in. Up close and personal, his love was confirmed. And get this. Jason paid in genuine Made in the USA dollars. He works for CUTCO Cutlery in Olean, New York, a real Made in the USA company. Cutco makes kitchen knives with the Forever Guarantee. And guys, they make Ka Bars. Jason is a Final Sharpener, a real craftsman. He's in a Modern Marvels videotape on Cutco's website, the guy slicing the paper. Selected from 425 employees to be one of six to appear with the CEO.

Three days later, Jason and Jane were safely home. They seemed happy together. Funny what a road trip will do. Would Jane even want to come back? I knew better than to ask. Sometimes, you've just gotta move on.

Have a great life, Jane. And thanks for the good times!

18

Sure, Get Your Kicks on Route 66, But Never Feel Blue on Highway 82!

November 2010

Thanksgiving. My family and I have received many blessings from living in the Sacramento Mountains and they are appreciated!

We all benefit from membership in a fine place like Cloudcroft. Per the Bible it's better to give than to receive. And all of us know receiving is fun. But haven't you found that when you give, like giving financially to your church, you receive back in abundance, especially when it's freely done and reward isn't expected?

Shouldn't we give back to our community, and not just money?

I've written about traveling on rivers in my 1957 Lone Star Starliner, a small cabin cruiser. It's not fancy but it's a conversation starter. How can I turn the interest that people show in it to Cloudcroft's advantage, I've wondered?

The boat is named "Miss Lucille", in honor of my mother who passed

away in 2008. Iris Lucille was an adventurous sort and would approve of such shenanigans.

To call attention to our village, I've placed "Cloudcroft, New Mexico" below my mother's name on the Starliner as my home port. People are surprised by a boat homeported in the mountains at almost 9,000 feet elevation. But not much about Cloudcroft surprises me.

Lisa King of the Chamber of Commerce provided me a quantity of the latest Cloudcroft Visitor's Guide. They're kept on board and handed out. We discussed another idea I have to promote Cloudcroft and she said she liked it. There are two possibilities. She either did like it or that was the quickest way to get me out of her office. For reasons of self-respect, I lean towards the former.

Allow me to digress to some experiences and knowledge. Once in Wichita Falls, Texas – the burning question in Wichita Falls being: Where are the falls? – I encountered that famous bad summertime weather. Hail pounded my oh-so-sweet 1978 Chevy El Camino. A panicked radio DJ announced a tornado at such and such intersection. I glanced at the nearest street sign. It was Such & Such Avenue.

East of Wichita Falls, crossing the Mississippi River from Arkansas… there's a new highway bridge to Greenville, Mississippi. I'll see the bottom of that bridge soon on a long river trip. A few miles ahead is Itta Bena, birthplace of blues musician B. B. King; the next town of Greenwood was a childhood home of actor Morgan Freeman.

Continue eastbound to Starkville, home of Mississippi State University. As a child of six, I perched in a shoe shine chair there for the first time. I felt uncomfortable with another human being shining my shoes, still don't like it much. We'd gone to Starkville for a football game.

Into Alabama, there's Montgomery where an old friend is the police chief. One crosses into Georgia over a river named the Chattahoochee,

and according to singer Alan Jackson, it's sometimes hotter there than a hootchie cootchie. Keep going and you're at Brunswick, Georgia, a major port on the Atlantic Ocean. I've been through Brunswick, but need to stop and visit beautiful St. Simons Island. Oh, keep going at St. Simons and you'll get wet.

The logical question: Well, so what? Okay, inquisitive one, glad you asked. The places mentioned are just a smidgen of those with a common link to Cloudcroft, New Mexico. Something you know very well, see every day. Give up?

U. S. Highway 82, of course! All Cloudcroftians recognize the western end of Highway 82 as the intersection where the person who just passed us on the double yellow is sitting one car ahead at the stop light in Alamogordo, at Highways 54 and 70. The eastern end is at Brunswick, Georgia, some 1,600 miles away, at Interstate 95. Elevation? Ten whole feet!

Ever gotten your kicks on Route 66? I have. Although U. S. Highway 66 ceased to exist as a real highway in 1985, it has such a tradition of having transported people westward from Chicago to California, it's still promoted. Merchants, too, continue to get their kicks from tourist dollars that come with that tradition.

A primary benefit of that highway's development was the growth of "mom and pop" businesses. Motels, cafes, service stations, gift shops. Many of them remain.

So what are we, chopped liver? Why need anyone feel blue if they're able to travel Route 82? From the White Sands of Alamogordo to the Atlantic Ocean! It's in a southern setting – ideal, for example, for springtime and fall RV travel, and includes New Mexico, Texas, Arkansas, Mississippi, Alabama and Georgia. And it remains complete, still in use. No remnants for good ole Highway 82!

Couldn't cities, towns, small communities along U. S. Highway 82 band together to promote travel of its entire length?

Sometime soon, I'll do the whole route, drop into Chambers of Commerce, travel and visitors bureaus, etc., along the way, discuss this idea. I'll keep a journal of interested persons and pass the results along to the Cloudcroft Chamber. Just maybe… And no, I won't be going in the boat. It'll be The Egg and me.

The Egg is a 1956 Shasta "canned ham" travel trailer, all 15 feet of it. My renovation of this little trailer included new light yellow paint and some over eagerness with red striping. The result? Looks like a big Easter egg. But, like Miss Lucille, it's a conversation starter!

Plain Jane, the '93 GMC pickup, with her friend The Egg, a '56 Shasta trailer, in Cloud County West.

This trip will be personal, since many people will see me in my bathrobe. The Egg has only a porta-potty, so RV parks with shower facilities will be sought. Please, you say. About three weeks should be needed for this adventure, hopefully done by year's end.

Will I ever feel blue on Route 82? I doubt it, and my wish and effort

will be that our community benefit from this small odyssey of ecstasy. Perhaps a RV magazine will be interested in a story, featuring Cloudcroft as the starting point. That's only logical, since it'll be downhill all the way to the Atlantic.

More on this later. Meanwhile, Happy Thanksgiving!

19

O' Christmas Tree –
Time to Gas Up the Bow Saw!

December 2010

"Twas the week before Christmas
and the trees were scared silly
They were dreading the coming
of Bow Saw Billy..."

All right! Time to head into the Lincoln National Forest for our Christmas tree. A great Cloudcroft tradition!

Real trees are beautiful, and smell so good inside your house. Your schnoz thinks it's in the great outdoors. And there's no bear poop on the floor.

Our recollections of Christmas as children center around a tree, don't they? Maybe a scraggly Charlie Brown model, but brightly colored ornaments and icicles, something underneath. And the anticipation of Christmas morning!

In my day, Edgar Bergen, the ventriloquist, had puppets Charlie McCarthy and Mortimer Snerd. Well-worn plaster statues of Charlie and Mortimer, each a foot tall, hid in our closet for 11 months, but escaped to stand under the Christmas tree each December.

I can close my eyes and be taken back in time to the aroma of the tree in the living room. Wait, I'll do that now, give me a second, please…

…Okay, nice! I'll stop another moment and think of actress Candice Bergen, Edgar's daughter. Hey, that was nice, too!

In a childhood Mississippi home recently, I couldn't recall where I'd slept. But I sure remembered exactly where we'd placed our Christmas tree.

My grandparents wouldn't themselves erect one. But in their parlor stood a small very old rickety table with a gray marble top. Had belonged to great grandma to the 3^{rd} power somebody. So annually I collected a little tree for the table top. My favorite Great Aunt Myrt would help decorate.

Sometimes what isn't under a tree may seem significant. In 1953, my dad worked in Honduras. The pesos were in short supply. At first glance Christmas morning, I selfishly thought: Is that all there is? But, honestly, I never suffered. Anyway, I love bananas.

Our holiday traditions are important. Our children usually continue them. And Christmas morning has always been the half day I'm content to just sit still on the couch, thinking how good life really is.

In a strange place – halfway around the world in the military as I was in Thailand years ago, maybe even in a prison cell - all those familiar things come flooding back.

Thank God for Christmas trees!

The whole forest is available for Christmas tree cutting to both Sacramento Mountain residents and those from the Land of Concrete. As a sheriff's deputy, guns and knives captured my attention, but some of my most frightening moments came when observing a woman, three children, a frozen dog and a man with a bow saw entering the woods. We welcome them, but a flatlander with a bow saw can be scary.

A frightened miniature tree with a bow saw, the WMD of the mountains!

In Russia Canyon, two adjacent trees were cut. One, a beautiful six footer, apparently was flawed, was abandoned. "Need a tree? We already have one," the landowner forlornly said. I took it to a Mayhill family, five kids. They were thrilled. The youngest is now a high school senior. We still occasionally talk about "our tree".

On Heliport Road, a 40 foot pine was cut and just the top removed, but soon abandoned a short distance away for the top of another 40 footer. My daughter's class used the discard at their Christmas dance. My poem, "The Top 10 Feet of a 40 Foot Tree", was published ten

years ago in the Mountain Monthly. Luckily for you, I didn't become the Poet Laureate of Otero County. I finished 13th in the contest. There were only 12 entries.

Amazingly, Christmas trees have been seen leaving the mountains tied on car tops, angel end/pointy end first. Someone, somewhere, had a Bad Hair Christmas.

Blue spruces are exceptional. I know of two "secret" growing places. One involves a mile drag back to your car. The other is about 15 miles away from the village where snow can be treacherous. Neither place is much visited.

In December 2004, a Highway 244 accident near Pine Campground resulted in a car over the side. Joe Mancillas of Cloudcroft Wrecker would have had to squash a small Charlie Browner to retrieve the vehicle. So it became my Christmas tree. It was beautiful because it didn't die a needless death, as did Deputy Bob Hedman a week later. It helped keep my spirits up during a very difficult time.

In Louisiana at Christmas in 2007, I visited my mother and stepfather. Both were ill, had no tree. But they did have that same rickety old table with the gray marble top from grandma's house. By then my mother was allergic to real trees, so I hiked over to the Dollar General forest. Result? A great holiday! The last with my folks, who both passed away the following year.

The most recent Lewis & Clark tree expedition in the Sacramentos for me was in December 2008. "Forget the bow saw," a friend said. "Use my chain saw. Much easier." Thus we toted it that mile to the perfect blue spruce. Pretty deep snow. To where the saw wouldn't start. So I cut that tree with the chain saw, used manually as a 10 pound bow saw. Followed by the mile drag, toting the saw. "Ha ha!" laughed my friend. Isn't it great to have good friends?

And it's a Christmas tree, not an Atheismas Tree or a Philosmas Tree or even a X-Mas Tree. It helps us celebrate the birth of Christ, not atheism, philosophy, or X. Remember His short life, and consider this song's words:

"He could have called 10,000 angels, to destroy the world, to set Him free. He could have called 10,000 angels… but He died alone, for you and me."

If you're not a Bow Saw Billy, there's always the Allsup's tree lot. And I may be there clandestinely selling the "only copy" of the treasure map to Hidden Spruce Tree Canyon. Raising cash to travel to my sister's home for the holidays. Her tree stands on the floor, but our grandmother's rickety little table is there, close by.

A Christmas tree is really love on a stick, isn't it? Enjoy yours this holiday season!

20

To Sail On the GYPSY WIND...

January 2011

Happy New Year! 2010 zipped by, didn't it? Did you empty your Bucket List of any items last year? Be sure and get some done in 2011!

My list is vague, a little hazy. There's a plan to hike the Appalachian Trail. But the last person I knew who did so got sick from a tick bite. Hmmm?

There's the very remote thought of attempting - notice "attempting" – a swim across the English Channel. Not as impossible as you might think. Only 13 miles at its narrowest point, the real challenge is the strong current on the French coast.

Another goal is a coast to coast bicycle ride. Through Cloudcroft, naturally. But recently I pedaled 17 miles on sudden impulse and it hurt. The part that hurt most? My rear end. Not a good sign.

Is one allowed to substitute unplanned Bucket List items - those that just suddenly appear - for others? I hope so. Here's one that fell into my lap recently.

Friends I've recruited for a long river trip turned the tide on me, pun intended. Bo and Smitty bought a 35 foot sailboat, the GYPSY WIND. It's in Florida. But they live in Nebraska and Texas, respectively, and need the boat back on the Texas coast. "Come along!" they said. Oh my. Decision time.

Have you aspired to be a sailor boy? To travel the high seas, brave sun, rain, wind and wave, lightning and storm? Well, me neither. But opportunity lost is usually opportunity regretted. Bo and Smitty have spent thousands and I have a chance for a free ride. A chance I can't turn down.

We've been working on the boat and it's ready. The three of us are novices, and needed an old salt to lead us. Then along came Dennis.

Bo, left, and Smitty prepare the Gypsy Wind at Hernando Beach, Florida, October 2010.

If "The Voyage of the Gypsy Wind" is a play, here are the players:

Bo. He's 58, a retired Assistant Chief of the San Antonio, Texas, Fire Department. Now lives in Nebraska helping care for his 92 year old

father-in-law. Bo was a San Antonio cop for six years, one of us. Bo's been to Cloudcroft once, spent a night at The Lodge.

In 1975, San Antonio officers James Bennett and George Copeland were fatally injured when struck by a car. They and a third policeman were handling a previous accident. The surviving cop dodged a flaming patrol car as it hurdled towards him. Then he comforted James and George as they died. He remained an officer for three more years until his son was born. Thinking he'd like to see the boy grow up, he transferred to the fire department where he ran in and out of burning buildings. Go figure. Yes, that third person was Bo, who's seen the elephant. He loves adventure. His motto? "Let's go!"

Smitty, 59. He worked as a Deputy Chief of the San Antonio Police Department. Was often the Chief's right hand man. Left the PD to become an aircraft traffic controller, but wisely returned. Preceded me as officer in charge of Special Operations – SWAT, hostage negotiations, the bomb squad, etc. A police chaplain recently told me: "Thank God for Smitty. He's my big brother. Helped me through many tribulations." Wait, isn't it supposed to be the other way around?

When I followed Smitty in police jobs, I used his operational plans because they were so professional. Why reinvent the wheel? I thought. He left the PD two years ago. He's visited Cloudcroft several times, stayed at Camp Chimney Springs and Mayhill RV parks.

Then there's Dennis, who retired from the SAPD in 1993. The consummate police officer, he spent 12 years in SWAT. Often first through the door against armed, barricaded subjects; to rescue hostages; to save lives. Dennis always had other interests, like sailing. For several years he's done boat deliveries throughout the Caribbean. Known as Captain D, he has a 70 foot sailboat of his own, the CORAL SEA.

Dennis' brother Mike was a San Antonio police detective, a friend. We lost Mike a few years back. Dennis, a Vietnam combat Marine, grew

up near the Florida Everglades, the setting of a 1989 book, "Porosus: Death in Forbidden Creek". A man named D. Alex Taws wrote that. I still have my copy. The astute reader will notice that Taws is SWAT spelled backwards. Mr. Taws – Dennis - is 64.

I have great faith in his abilities, so when he signed on, I joined as the fourth player. Once again a cabin boy, my accepted fate. At 67, the Old Man and The Sea.

We've waited out hurricane season, and weather permitting, will launch on Saturday, December 11th. Our planned course is straight across the Gulf of Mexico, 900 miles from near Tampa, Florida, to Corpus Christi, Texas. We'll usually be about 150 to 200 miles offshore. Sailing time anywhere from four and one half days up.

Am I worried? Well, yes. My biggest concern is seasickness. I don't want to be a burden to others. And forget the cute comments like "shark bait", "knucklehead", or the old favorite, "be sure to spell my name correctly in your will". Other friends have already covered those.

The Mountain Monthly will receive daily e-mail alerts from my SPOT GPS satellite messenger showing our condition and position on a Google map.

This is the first part of a two part story, of course, and I'll conclude Part I by saying I love Cloudcroft and the Sacramento Mountains and have firm plans to write Part II.

Thank God for guys like James and George and Mike and Otero County Deputy Bob Hedman who put it all on the Thin Blue Line and left it there, and for leaving us dinosaurs behind for a while to enjoy life.

May the Good Lord keep you safe as we ask He'll keep us. Have a great New Year, and don't neglect your own Bucket List!

21

Part II, Voyage of the GYPSY WIND!

February 2011

Part I last month was about a planned sailboat trip from near Tampa, Florida, to Corpus Christi, Texas. Friends Bo, Smitty and Dennis invited me to sail across the Gulf of Mexico in the GYPSY WIND, a Hunter 35 footer. Weather permitting, we'd start December 11th. We didn't. Thick fog at the last minute.

Glancing at a mirror while delayed, I wondered: What from Cloudcroft could go along to help avoid mayhem for guys like us? My ball cap's cross-eyed moose stared back as if to say: Hey, take me! OK, then.

On December 15th, at 8:30 AM during high tide, we got underway. It was 25 degrees. Within half a minute we were stuck.

The canal to the Gulf hadn't been dredged lately. We were grounded four more times. Once it almost wasn't temporarily. Harrowing. Finally, open water!

It was beautiful, sunny, fairly calm. A Grand Banks yacht crossed our path. Headed for Key West? We began a 24/7 operation. Perpetual

motion. Someone always at the helm. My night shift would be 3:00 AM to 6:00 AM, plus some daylight hours.

Mr. Murphy came along, of course. The depth finder malfunctioned. We cut a wire, problem fixed. Smooth sailing. Later we learned that same wire controlled the compass light. Oops. We couldn't see the compass, and a flashlight was occasionally necessary. Not good for night vision, or a person with just two hands.

By morning, completely overcast, Small Craft Warnings issued. We were 150 miles off Panama City, Florida. Winds were 20 plus knots, seas 12 to 15 feet. Forget calm. We crashed and banged about the cabin. I demolished a full-length mirror. A door knob wrenched off in Smitty's hand. A cockpit door and the oven door were smashed. Dennis' head took a good whack on a bulkhead. We were tossed around like rag dolls.

Off Panama City, Florida, Smitty navigates westbound through 15 foot waves!

One time the sail "luffed" - lost wind - popped and slapped violently! It took everyone to make an emergency adjustment. The sail was frayed, but it wasn't destroyed. A close call.

Another time, Smitty and Bo were in the cabin, trying to rest. Suddenly they bolted topside! "What'd we hit?" they nervously asked. Dennis and I were clueless, but apparently the hull had impacted some object. Several tense moments passed as we checked for a leak or other damage, nothing found.

The next two days, wave height decreased to 8 to 10 feet. Meanwhile, an old college friend, Ralph, joined Mr. Murphy. My worst fear realized. Seasickness! For 24 hours, I was the Puke King. With dehydration in mind, Granola bars and water saved my bacon. Hungry, then, the rest of the way. Go figure!

Off Mobile, Alabama, through a cold front, rain squalls. Steering shifts ended with water squishing in our shoes. No other vessels or land were sighted until large cargo carriers the third night off the boot heel of Louisiana, as those ships entered the Mississippi River channel.

Mr. Murphy remained. We'd lost our fuel gauge, and had a fuel leak. Luckily, diesel. The sharks we'd seen twice felt differently but we didn't want to swim. So we sailed to Grand Isle, Louisiana, to top up our diesel and ourselves. To then, my one hot meal had been oatmeal so the rib platter at the Starfish Café was amazing. We inhaled our food.

Lisa helped with transportation. Lisa's mother ran the Starfish. Grand Isle people aren't shy. Lisa's mother's greeting to a friend: "Hey, where you been, you bald-headed S. O. B.?" Just like Cloudcroft! We slept in real beds, took showers on sea legs, watched football. Ahhh, civilization.

Six AM, grounded again. Waited four hours for high tide. The Sand Dollar Marina guy could have warned us, but doesn't like "blow boats".

The previous customer had spent a thousand bucks, we spent a hundred. We sailed southwest, into the offshore Louisiana oil patch.

We passed near where the BP Deepwater Horizon blew up last summer. One of the Forgotten Eleven killed was a young man from my Mississippi hometown. We considered the hazards of workers on the hundreds of rigs we saw. Good people just trying to make a living.

We traveled westward about 60 miles out. Through a maze, a giant ocean garden erector set of metallic vegetables feeding the American appetite for oil. Helicopters overhead, work boats nearby.

By night, a full moon. Following or preceding a lunar trail on the water when it wasn't cloudy, we steered carefully through the network of rigs, waves 8 to 10 feet. In the darkness, Bo and I fought the Battle of the Unlit Compass. The bow swung quickly, left, right! We'd pick a faint platform light some 10 miles distant, five degrees to port off the bow, steer towards it for an hour and a half. Passing it, we'd find another, 10 miles farther on.

"Oooo..." "Eeeeeeeeeeeeee eeeeeeeeeeeeeeeeeeeee..." from all around, over and over. Unmanned structures have audible ghost-like alarms that sound for three seconds, are quiet for twenty. Eerie in the blackness.

Into waters off Texas. Red lights, green lights, white lights, a few shrimp boats dragging nets. Which way were they moving? Radio chatter. Intense. At shift's end, we fell exhausted into sleep, but just for an hour or two. An endurance contest that wore at you. All of us lost weight. Eight pounds for me.

Day Seven. 4:30 AM, about 30 miles off Galveston. An oil rig suddenly disappeared, fog! And the wind died. Bo and I woke the others, all hands needed. Motoring carefully, hearing foghorns, we ran out of fuel! We had spare cans, refueled in giant swells, the weight of the keel

rolling us drastically side to side. Luckily the engine restarted without repriming.

We carefully followed buoys into the seaport. Reminiscent of landing an aircraft under instrument conditions. We'd see just the hulls of cargo ships, their superstructures hidden in earthbound clouds.

We'd changed our destination to Kemah, Texas, near Houston. Dennis knows the marina owner. There's an amusement park, and we sailed northwest across Galveston Bay towards a brightly lit Ferris wheel. The garish lights were in sharp contrast to previous nights. About 7:30 PM, December 22nd, we passed quietly between staring groups of Christmas visitors along the waterfront. A little in shock, maybe. We, not them.

Was God out there on the water? We prayed for a safe journey, and had one. Trouble came but left. We looked at a full moon, its light dancing on the waves. The Milky Way dazzled us. We saw many fins but most were frolicking and friendly, dolphins and porpoises. The big dipper was directly above, and blessings poured liberally from it. Magical and mystical scenes.

Could all we saw have been created accidentally? No way.

When we left Florida, Captain D said: "I'll get you there safely." He, the Good Lord, good luck and the GYPSY WIND did just that. It was sad to leave her alone at the dock. We learned to trust her, to believe that each time she'd bury her bow in the waves, every time she'd keel over, she'd come back up. Gypsy always did. She's a good little ship.

Give me a lighted compass, and I'll sail anywhere with those guys. It was my best adventure yet.

It was also the first documented crossing of the Gulf of Mexico by a cross-eyed moose. You, Cloudcroft, were part of my crew, and you are appreciated!

22

Gotta Go Gotta Go Gotta Go Right Now!

April 2011

The Pine Stump Mall restroom was mentioned here recently. Bathrooms are an unusual topic of discussion but they're important. Several times a day.

If one dips deeply enough into the well of ideas, someday black water appears in the bucket. So here we are. Potty stories. Ughhh!

Can't you imagine the first cavewoman saying: "Charlie dear, can you take that outside? Good grief!" "Sorry, babe. Musta been the skunk dinner last night. Oh, put corn cobs on the shopping list. We're running short."

Growing up in a small Mississippi town shortly after Dinosaur Days, it was my luck to have indoor plumbing. But my grandparents didn't, until the middle 1950s. And a lot of my childhood was spent at their place.

Those outdoor privies? Spiders were a constant threat. Black widows ruled the roost. Could bite you where you didn't want to be bitten. As you were browsing the Sears catalog. Yes, it was really there, and guess what the last section to go – no pun intended – was? Ladies' lingerie. Figure that out on your own.

Inside my grandparents' home for overnight use were chamber pots tucked away under the beds. We called 'em Thundermugs. My dear Great Aunt Myrt emptied those each morning. And she managed to keep a terrific sense of humor. Imagine that!

The favorite terroristic threat at school then? Cherry bombs flushed down the toilet. The distinctive "Whoomph!" sound deep in the bowels of the building was unmistakable. And without restrooms, what would we have done to escape from class? "Teacher, I've gotta go. Now!"

Anyone remember Feen-a-mint chewing gum laxative? It was orange colored, actually tasted pretty good. My younger cousin Don constantly pilfered my Juicy Fruit. Finally exasperated, I restocked with Feen-a-mint. With my encouragement, he took the whole pack. Mississippi has gotten over it, but Louisiana still remembers the family's return trip home to New Orleans as "The Day the Pelicans Laughed". Set a state record for the number of toilet stops. My Aunt Annette still disliked me when she died.

Different countries have different customs. My year in Thailand introduced me to bidets, common due to early French influence. A less traveled friend thought it was a funny place to put a water fountain.

A police officer's use of a restroom is challenging because of the amount of equipment carried that must be removed. The Tools of Ignorance, per a cadet school instructor. The gun, extra ammo, nightstick, flashlight, buck knife, handcuffs, pepper spray, radio, emergency donut, etc.

Once, on duty but having lunch at a Texas barbeque restaurant, Mother Nature and not the police dispatcher called me. The bathroom was in a separate, non air- conditioned building. A rather large room which was summertime hot.

Moving in slow motion to avoid perspiring, the Tools were left in a far corner. Then a bee flew in through a vent in the ceiling. A very large, very unhappy bee. It dive-bombed repeatedly during my desperate attempt to do what one does in a bathroom then retrieve my gear and put it back on.

Returning inside drenched in sweat, my partner in the air conditioned café was curious as to just why it was so hot in the restroom. "It would bee too hard to explain," I said, adding to my mystique.

While enthroned at home on a later occasion, a mouse suddenly and unexpectedly darted out from behind the commode, between my legs. It was a startling place to see a mouse do such a thing, especially in daylight.

That little rat frantically reversed course and disappeared behind the toilet through a tiny crack in the wall where the baseboard met the tub. After a minute to recover, I loaded my .22 rifle with rat shot. Yep, stayed in the bathroom and watched that small mouse hole for maybe 30 minutes with my gun aimed.

Its nose would occasionally appear, but blasting the mouse back into the wall where it would remain and really stink up the place wasn't desirable. So a waiting game continued until it was well outside the crack. At least it appeared so.

Good plan but no banana. Pulling the trigger, the mouse disappeared. Back inside the west wall, of course, facing the afternoon summer sun. For three months, it seemed that wall would have to be dismantled. Oh boy. The mummified remains most likely still exist. The neighbors

believed King Tut was stored in our house. Everybody was mad at me. The odor eventually went away.

During World War II, Camp Van Dorn near Centreville, Mississippi, was an Army training base. Centreville is close to Liberty, my hometown. The camp was named for Confederate General Earl Van Dorn, who loved two things. The cavalry and women. Wounded several times in battle, his ills —at least the womanizing portion - were finally cured by a doctor in 1863. The physician was a jealous husband who shot Van Dorn in the back of the head.

Touring the camp museum recently, a snapshot of a soldier sitting alone in the "head" caught my eye. If you're ever visiting my house and use the bathroom (don't forget a dime for the door), you'll find that picture framed, over the commode. "Head time" can be one of the rare moments of privacy in a military training environment.

Camp Van Dorn's units went to Europe, fought in the Battle of the Bulge. Is the identity of the soldier in the photograph known? Did he live throughout the war? Museum curator Patricia Rogers says his name is uncertain, but of the two possibilities, both men survived. It's one of the bestselling copies of a photo the museum has.

During my police career, death had frequently taken place in a bathroom, in various ways. Have you been to Graceland, Elvis Presley's mansion in Memphis, Tennessee? Touring there sometime back, my curiosity was drawn to Elvis' restroom. It was from the floor of that room that he left the building a final time, possibly from a heart attack, maybe from a drug overdose. He was just 42.

May the Good Lord bless and keep you safe, even in the john! But gentlemen, please…put the seat down when done. And the tissue should always come off the top of the roll, never the bottom.

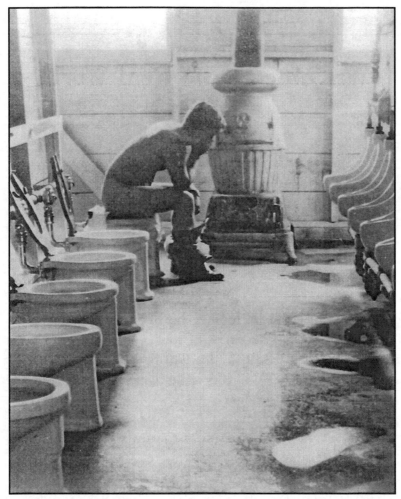

In a rare moment of solitude, this WWII soldier may be thinking of home.

Use caution! If the Charmin is gone and you find a Sears catalog, you've been seriously transported through a time warp to a place you really shouldn't be. Don't squeeze the catalog, or tease the spiders.

23

Welcome To the Real World!

May 2011

Cloudcroft High School, the mother ship of our little mountain galaxy, will soon blast a whole new crew of rookie astronauts into the lofty heavens known as the Real World. No more coddling. What career choices will they make? Will they go to college or begin work right away? Will they join the military?

It's an exciting time but a scary time for many.

We wise old owls who place ourselves as gurus on the mountain top always have advice, don't we? Been There, Done That. For those going to college, here's something learned the hard way by Yours Truly. Three simple words. "Do the homework."

High school seemed easy, but college ended all that. If they had a probation named it, I tried it. Attendance, Scholastic, Whatever. A former non-achiever high school friend was doing well at LSU. I wasn't. "How do you do it, Bobby?" "I just do the homework," he replied.

Wow! What a brilliant, original idea! That thought had never occurred

to me. Mixing a bit of elbow grease into those words - it worked. Things became much simpler.

Of course the bills must be paid …hold onto your hat…since nothing is really free. But life's too brief to make a career choice that one cannot stand, and there actually is more to it than money. No matter what the equivalent of Monday morning is, one should look forward to returning to work, and not hate the thought.

As a police officer, my Monday morning was often Wednesday night at 10 PM, but I don't recall ever dreading going back after my days off.

A few years ago, a teacher asked me to address high school seniors at a pre-graduation event. Perplexed, the best idea that surfaced was to quote my favorite poem, "The Calf-Path". Mr. Foss, the author, was a New Hampshire fellow who wrote things of the "common man" variety. He died way back in 1911, but his wisdom – through poetry –still applies 100 years later. Okay, call me cheap, but this poetic offering is freely given to CHS students.

Undoubtedly, there are more exciting things for Bear grads to do than peruse this column. So for those older adults reading who receive an invitation mandating an expensive graduation gift, here's how to satisfy that obligation for just fifty cents. The cost of a Mountain Monthly. Oh, you're welcome! Just pass along the poem. (Adding a $20 yuppie food stamp might not be a bad idea, though.)

The Calf-Path
by Sam Walter Foss (1858-1911)

One day, through the primeval wood,
A calf walked home, as good calves should;
But made a trail all bent askew,
A crooked trail, as all calves do.

Since then three hundred years have fled,
And, I infer, the calf is dead.
But still he left behind his trail
And thereby hangs my moral tale.

The trail was taken up next day
By a lone dog that passed that way
And then a wise bellwether sheep
Pursued the trail o'er vale and steep,
And drew the flock behind him, too,
As good bellwethers always do.

And from that day, o'er hill and glade,
Through those old woods a path was made,
And many men wound in and out,
And dodged and turned and bent about
And uttered words of righteous wrath
Because 'twas such a crooked path.

But still they followed — do not laugh —
The first migrations of that calf,
And through this winding wood-way stalked
Because he wobbled when he walked.

This forest path became a lane,
That bent, and turned, and turned again.
This crooked lane became a road,
Where many a poor horse with his load
Toiled on beneath the burning sun,
And traveled some three miles in one.

And thus a century and a half
They trod the footsteps of that calf.

The years passed on in swiftness fleet.
The road became a village street,
And this, before men were aware,
A city's crowded thoroughfare,
And soon the central street was this
Of a renowned metropolis.
And men two centuries and a half
Trod in the footsteps of that calf.

Each day a hundred thousand rout
Followed that zigzag calf about,
And o'er his crooked journey went
The traffic of a continent.
A hundred thousand men were led
By one calf near three centuries dead.

They follow still his crooked way,
And lose one hundred years a day,
For thus such reverence is lent
To well-established precedent.

A moral lesson this might teach
Were I ordained and called to preach;
For men are prone to go it blind
Along the calf-paths of the mind,
And work away from sun to sun
To do what other men have done.

They follow in the beaten track,
And out and in, and forth and back,
And still their devious course pursue,
To keep the path that others do.

They keep the path a sacred groove,
Along which all their lives they move;
But how the wise old wood-gods laugh,
Who saw the first primeval calf!

The message is clear. Be creative. Don't simply follow the herd. Cut your own path through the woods. Be an innovator, not one who simply follows in the hoof prints of original thinkers. Our time on this earth is short, really. Make the most of it!

There's no sound more regretful down the road than the muffled laugh of a wood-god behind your back.

We were all young once, weren't we? Remember your own high school graduation? Could we imagine life years from then? No way. Cap-and-gown time for me was 1961. So, yes, this is my 50th reunion year. Elementary school classmates in Mississippi invited me to their recent get-together. We had a great time! My friends Mary, Linda and Mary headed to the water tower to climb it once again. They found it blocked, but their grandchildren will be proud to know they tried.

Oregon (middle school) and Louisiana (high school) classmates will find me happily in their company later this year for their 50th reunions, as well.

Good luck to the Cloudcroft Class of 2011! May God bless you with long, successful and happy lives, with Him included, and may all of you meet again in 50 years to celebrate!

Whatever you choose, don't forget the magic formula: "Do the homework."

24

Way to Go, George Collins!

June 2011

It's quite likely you've accomplished some really good things in life someplace else, things we in Cloudcroft should know about but don't. Some people just don't talk much about themselves.

Recently a grandson gave me something I didn't want. The crud. Knocked my socks off for a week. That down time, though, provided opportunity. Allowed me to begin a long-delayed memoir. Something I'll probably call "Foxtrot, We're On The Way!", about the five years I flew police helicopters with the San Antonio, Texas, Police Department.

Doing so was a dream come true job, quite the butt kick! Oops, did I say that? Excuse me.

Many of you knew George Collins from the Cloudcroft Chamber of Commerce. I did too. But I also knew George during his years as a dispatcher with the Otero County Sheriff's Office.

Heck, George and I knew each other so well at the OCSO, we even

had an argument or two. But we got beyond that, back into the friendship zone.

I knew he was retired from the Los Angeles County, California, Sheriff's Office. Also that he'd worked in their helicopter unit. We had that chopper business in common and traded some war stories. It was something we'd both really enjoyed.

Cloudcroft's very own George Collins during his flying days in California.

But was George too modest? There was something he never told me. A good thing that he had done.

The City of Lakewood, California, part of Los Angeles County, had the first day and night police helicopter program in the United States, indeed the first in the world. An 18 month test was conducted during 1966-67. During that time, major crimes decreased more than 10% when a helicopter was overhead.

By 1968 Lakewood was going full blast, has been ever since. Progressive police departments, San Antonio amongst those, studied the early results, and started its own aerial law enforcement unit in 1971. Both agencies used the small Hughes 300 model chopper. I became involved in Texas in 1975, and remember studying the Lakewood airborne patrol strategy.

George's unit was called Sky Knight. In San Antonio, the letter "F" was the last position of registrations affixed to our aircraft. That letter in aviation jargon is Foxtrot, so we became known that way. Much later our name was changed to Blue Eagle, which remains to the present.

Lakewood, California, has an Award of Valor program. Here's a quote from the city's website about that award:

"Lakewood heroes are honored though an annual Award of Valor event. Lakewood's tradition of honoring public safety professionals, active volunteers, and community members reflects an enduring Lakewood value: Giving support to those who sacrifice to keep our neighborhoods safe. A special Award of Valor luncheon is held each fall.

From the first days of the new city in 1954, Lakewood residents, sheriff's deputies and firefighters have cooperated in securing the lives and property of residents, business owners, and visitors. In the process, they've built strong bonds of trust and respect that work to sustain Lakewood's remarkable quality of life.

Another Lakewood website contains an article titled: "Sky Knight: 40 Years of Aerial Law Enforcement". Since we studied Sky Knight as we established our operating procedures in San Antonio, I was recently researching that information for the memoir I'm working on, and stumbled across the following direct quote:

"Case study: River rescue. In early 1991, as unexpected spring runoff poured through the region's flood control channels, Sky Knight rescued two boys who had been swept away while bike riding in the San Gabriel River bed. Landing downstream, Sky Knight Pilot Carl Cortez and his observer, Deputy George Collins, formed a human chain to pull the youngsters from the water. More than once the force of the flow nearly brought down both men as they struggled to rescue the two boys. Finally, they brought the exhausted and cold youngsters to

safety. For their courage and quick thinking, pilot Cortez and observer Collins received the 1991 Lakewood Award of Valor."

Hey, that's OUR George! An Award of Valor winner, and we knew nothing about it.

Folks, that was a serious honor. From my experience and training, what George and his partner encountered was a matter of life or death. Landing in such a situation endangers the public and the aircraft. The main rotor blades continue to rotate for a long time afterwards. "Buzz saw" would be a good substitute name for the tail rotor, which turns at several thousand RPMs. Landing on an uneven surface is especially hazardous, as blade tips dip closer to the ground.

Time permitting, a ground unit or fire department rescue squad would be summoned. The Hughes 300 will carry only the two-person crew, cannot transport people away. Landing changes a three-quarter million dollar specialized piece of equipment to what can be done with a regular motor vehicle. Elimination of the aerial observation platform may cause others to be endangered. The helicopter's advantages are gone. Such landings are made only in extreme circumstances - immediate danger to life or limb - when there's no alternative. That's the official take, the policy. In real life? You do what you gotta do.

George Collins gave years to public service in law enforcement, and more years to public service at the Cloudcroft Chamber of Commerce. (As to the latter, so did his wife and daughter). Please say "Thank you!" to the Collins family next time you see them, they deserve it.

And George, you did good in Cal-i-forn-i-a! Way to go! And you never told us about it. Thanks for your courageous act. Your personal support was always appreciated too, as was that of your colleagues out West. Here's hoping somebody slaps you. A gentle congratulatory one, on the back.

May the Good Lord bless you and yours during retirement!

25

Independence Day Reflections on the Coming of Independence

August 2011

Between 1840 – 1860, half a million people moved westward along the Oregon Trail from Missouri. "Oregon or Bust!" they shouted.

That sentiment was repeated during the Great Depression.

"Oregon or Bust!" we joked in 1955, moving there. Why did we go? My father was a millwright who maintained a sawmill. Lumber, no longer the king in Mississippi, was at least still a prince out west. So he went for work.

We arrived in Ashland, Oregon, during a treacherous snowstorm, over the Green Springs pass from Klamath Falls. Our first such storm. Sighting Ashland's lights through the snow, far down in the valley, was exciting! It was much like seeing the lights of Tularosa from below the tunnel on U. S. Highway 82.

Our little Ford had all our worldly goods, plus two adults and my sister

and me. And the parrot, his cage, and our dog. I'd been wedged into the back seat for the 2,500 mile trip.

On the way, Truth or Consequences, New Mexico... What a different name, I thought! We had our first Mexican food there.

Folks from at least four Mississippi towns took that Oregon Trail, beginning in 1949. My family only stayed two and one half years, just enough to get me through junior high school.

For this shy Southern country boy, it was a serious change of cultures. But being a Westerner turned out to be a good thing.

Junior high, now middle school, is a coming of age time, isn't it? My teenage years were just starting. And yes, I'd have started to grow up anywhere, but it happened in Oregon.

Ashland, now a town of more than 20,000 persons, had only 8,000 then.

A coming of age... Remember when your engine started idling faster, and I don't mean the one in your Ford, or Chevy? When a kiss went from an Uggghhh! (grandma) to a Hmmmm?, maybe even an Ohhh Yeah! (Member of the opposite sex your same age ?) The little hairs on the back of your neck stood up?

The yearbook shows me holding my girlfriend at a school dance. "He's not Dodg'ing her," the caption reads. I was learning to tread softly and carefully, though. Her father, Mr. Dodge, was my math teacher.

At the Varsity Theatre, teens discovered how deeply we could snuggle into a seat, ever vigilant for our mortal enemy. The usher, Movie Cop.

I thought of...cars!...girls!... Both parents worked, so my hours were becoming more private. My bicycle took me to forbidden places, to hopeful places.

Bob, a classmate, had come from Alaska where his father had been a bush pilot. Bob regaled me with flying stories. I caught the fever. The five mile pedal to the airport became routine. Out there, I'd hold onto the fence, hoping someone would offer me a plane ride.

It never happened, but I never quit holding on or hoping.

Ashland at its essence is a liberal community, a midpoint between Los Angeles and Seattle. A Starbucks coffee kind of place. It's home to the world-famous Oregon Shakespearian Festival. As a young boy, I played in the old outdoor theatre, watched dress rehearsals of The Bard's plays.

The designer of San Francisco's Golden Gate Park planned Lithia Park, Ashland's centerpiece. Ashland Creek flows through it. In the 1950s, lumberjack contests, like the ones held in Cloudcroft, were staged in the park.

Logrolling wasn't the event to lose. A large flock of ducks lived in the park's small pond, ducks that weren't careful with their hygiene.

Ashland High School's Class of '61 had its 50th reunion over the recent Fourth of July weekend. I've stayed in touch with people I shared that coming of age time with. Somehow, we all survived it.

They're good, solid Americans, many educators among them. Southern Oregon University, the local institution of higher learning, trained many teachers during our college days.

It's said Ashland almost died in the 1970s, was down to three or four stores downtown. But the hippies came, with their head shops and tattoo parlors. Then the yuppies discovered Ashland, bought the hippies' stores one by one. Now the town is a lively center of the arts, plays, and higher priced homes.

The hippies saved the town, the locals say. Good for the hippies.

Our class had a float in the July 4th parade. We couldn't throw candy but handed out a bunch. The crowd yelled: "Go Bears!" Was I back in Cloudcroft? No, Grizzly Peak dominates the eastern horizon, and AHS teams are the Grizzlies. We had a great time!

For what I consider a liberal community, Mayor John Stromberg's comments at day's end were thought- provoking. The Daily Tidings quoted him as follows: "As long as I can remember the Fourth of July has been about the past…But in July of 2011, I find myself wondering if our system of government actually can work for a country of some 330 million people…I feel that democracy's best hope may be at the local level, in small towns like Ashland…Here, in so many ways we are trying to make democracy work… On this level I feel much more confident."

Are even liberal communities becoming as upset about the direction of our national government as more conservative ones are?

Finally, all quiet on the Western front, so I sought out the old mill site where as a youth, I swept sawdust, cut grass with a sling blade. Modern homes now cover the area, but there's a beautiful private park with a small pond. It's our old mill pond from the 1950s!

I trespassed momentarily to sit on its banks and reflect. The name of the group of houses? Mill Pond Subdivision. And the street that takes you there? Mill Pond Road.

Many Californians have retired to Ashland and live in that subdivision. Many might be surprised to learn the center of their turf is a legacy of Mississippi rednecks from more than 50 years ago.

Thank you, God, for good friends, great memories and a present day life that allows me to make new ones. Your part in this, Cloudcroft, is always appreciated!

26

The Soldier on the Mantle

October 2011

To me, in my childhood, he was simply the Soldier on the Mantle.

The mantle wasn't in a sad home. But I wondered about the photo of the man in uniform, and my one question about him, when I was about seven, was met with sadness

"Who's that?" I'd asked. "That was Albert," my Great Aunt Fannie told me. "He died in the war." WWII. Somehow I came to believe he'd died in France during the Normandy invasion.

Many people have soldiers on the fireplace mantle. Perhaps you do. Maybe yours served in later wars, like Vietnam, Iraq or Afghanistan. Maybe they're your sons or grandsons. Could be they're young women.

Fortunately, most come home safely. I hope yours did, or do. Their service is appreciated. They're the reason we live in a free country.

Aunt Fannie was an "old maid" until age 50. But Albert's mother died, and somehow Mr. Neyland and my aunt met and married. Thus my

aunt became Albert's stepmother. They farmed and ranched way out in the Mississippi boonies.

Going there was through a gap, up and over a hill, down into a hollow where there was a creek bed, through another gap, then up another long hill to their home. It may have been a mile off the main road. Maybe it was only a quarter of a mile and another three-fourths mile of faulty memory. It's been 40 years since my last visit.

A gap? In some places they call them a wire gate. It's a temporary gate, really. Just an opening in the fence closed with a collection of wires and sticks.

Temporary? A friend once said the most permanent structure on a farm was a temporary barn. Gaps are like that. They stay a long time. In my youth, the youngest occupant who was physically able to handle the gap exited the car, opened and closed it. Gap duty.

That's why gapsters always campaigned for a little brother or sister, I suppose.

But going to my Uncle Wiley's and Aunt Fannie's house was fun. Surprisingly, they were among the first to have television. So we visited on Saturdays when the best TV shows were on.

There, like birds on a wire, we'd line up on the couch and watch the Hit Parade, I Led 3 Lives, the Loretta Young Show. I remember Loretta swishing in through a door in the opening scene, her full evening dress flying around in a circle. The Soldier on the Mantle silently watched with us. Though still curious about him, I kept quiet.

There were other things I liked there. A Dodge truck, a Ford tractor, two horses, and a spring. The backyard was full of turkeys, some of the toms mean, and I didn't like them. They'd chase you. Annually, a couple of the meanest ones were Guests of Honor at Thanksgiving.

When one was in pursuit, it made you feel better to know you'd be eating him later, something the turkey didn't seem to understand.

The Soldier had driven that Dodge truck or that Ford tractor, or similar ones, before he left for Army training in 1943. Horses live a long time so he may have ridden them, too.

Once my first wife and I were visiting, and she was petting a horse. They were friendly, but were seldom ridden, and then by someone they knew. "Suppose I could ride one?" she asked. "Of course. See how gentle they are," I said. So she hopped up on one, bareback. The horse, insulted, promptly bucked her off.

Not one to curse, nevertheless she shouted: "You SOB!" as she flew by me horizontally, Superwoman-style. And her comment wasn't for the horse. I still recall getting The Look. I think it was all mentioned later in divorce court.

All this has been sitting on a brain shelf for a very long time. Recently, researching old newspaper articles in Mississippi for a project, I glanced at a paper dated October 1, 1948, and noticed the following:

"Funeral services were held for Albert G. Neyland at the Presbyterian Church Tuesday afternoon, September 28, the pastor, Reverend I. O. Alexander, officiating, assisted by Dr. C. M. Savage, pastor of the Baptist Church.

Albert, the son of Mr. Wiley Neyland and the late Mrs. Neyland, was killed in action at or near Casino, Italy, January 14, 1944. He entered the service of our country May 3, 1943. He was 21 years of age, that age when life is looked forward to as a glorious future, but he paid the supreme sacrifice for his country.

He was born and raised in Liberty and attended school here, so it is

fitting that he rest in peace here. He was a member of the Presbyterian Church, having accepted Christ as Savior early in life

He is survived by his father and stepmother of Liberty, two brothers, Harry and Carl and one sister, Bonnie, all of Baton Rouge, three nephews and one niece, also of Baton Rouge.

Military rites were conducted at the graveside, sweet and impressive."

By pure chance I learned more about the Soldier than I'd ever known. He was killed in Italy, not France, just prior to four great battles the Allies fought to advance north past the great hilltop abbey of Monte Casino, built in AD524. The first such battle officially started January 17, 1944. The Germans had put up stiff resistance beforehand as Allied forces moved into place.

Why was his funeral service held in 1948 when he was killed in action during 1944? My guess is that his body was buried in Italy, later exhumed and returned to the United States for proper services.

It's as if the Soldier on the Mantle found a way to speak after all this time. I wish he knew he was remembered, even years ago by a young boy who silently wondered about his fate. I wish he'd come home safely to eat those Thanksgiving turkeys with us, since they'd probably chased him too.

There was always a mental place for him at the table, although it was never talked about.

27

Remembering the Veterans from the Land of Bad Things

November 2011

As of today, I'm declaring myself a Vietnam Veteran, 40 years later. Why now? Three days ago, I attended an event and saw a friend, Joe, wearing a Vietnam Veteran's ball cap, with U. S. Air Force on it. "I can do that," I thought.

In my mind, the Marines - the Army infantrymen and helicopter crews - the Navy river patrol sailors – and okay, the Air Force fighter pilots – are the real Vietnam Veterans. Between the lines, read "combat". You know, the people who had a swarm of hornets buzzing past their heads. The guys who saw friends stung by those hornets. The folks who slogged through the jungle, boated the rivers, dodged the missiles.

Vietnam. The Land of Bad Things, my old friend Bob Hedman called it. He'd been there.

SSgt Robert Hedman, Jr., US Army (retired), Vietnam veteran.
Bob was a military policeman and K-9 handler.

Many soldiers were draftees. The draft motivated us all. If you were healthy, a t-shirt emblazoned with a bull's eye awaited you. It was the Target store logo look.

I had no hankering to be in the military, but the draft mandated that. In high school, I hung around with smart people, as their court jester. My smart friends went to college, thus so did I. It was a temporary escape from the draft, but if you didn't enroll in ROTC, the draft enrolled in you, right after graduation.

So I became a young officer, assigned to a unit that trained F-4 fighter aircrews. Everyone was headed to Vietnam. Our country was headed that direction. The world seemed bent on the domino theory with a lot of it headed the direction of communism.

I respected political leaders then more than now, but didn't know that LBJ, for example, micromanaged the war by personally picking bombing targets. If his military advisor didn't agree, he didn't change the targets, he changed military advisors.

My country had given me great advantages from my birth and I felt I should be over there, since many of my friends were over there. So in spite of having been married all of 90 days, I volunteered. One didn't volunteer for Vietnam, one volunteered for Southeast Asia which was a way of saying Vietnam in two words.

To this day, my wife then still doesn't know I volunteered.

Imagine my surprise when my orders soon arrived. Thailand? I was assigned to a fighter wing that flew F-105 Thunderchiefs, primarily over North Vietnam.

I worked in a support role, seven days a week. But I traveled around Thailand on a small Honda motorcycle when time permitted; looking at ancient temples, the world's largest banyan tree. Air Force planes took me to places like the Philippines and Taiwan. Bangkok fascinated me.

When in Bangkok, I'd encounter the American kids – I was a ripe old 24 or 25, they were just 18 or so – who were doing the real fighting. And I don't mean just in the Bangkok nightclubs, I'm talking the serious jungle stuff. They received leave for only two weeks, and seeing them made me feel a little guilty.

It was just the luck of the draw, I suppose. For every one person in

actual combat, there were 10 behind the lines in support roles. And for every soldier in a firefight, there were supposedly many who never fired their weapons, just kept their heads down. But nevertheless, they were there, in a foxhole with God, no atheists to be found.

And remember that mortars are designed to come straight down, into foxholes.

Having jumped into a few of them later, in the police business, I can report having found no atheists in my foxholes, either. I was glad to have God in there with me, still am.

But as military matters go, I've never felt quite worthy to sport the tag, Vietnam Veteran, since to me that implies combat, or at least having been in the country. It was weird. I was in Vietnam once, but never set foot in Vietnam. We landed during the Tet Offensive, but weren't allowed off the plane. I flew over Vietnam en route to Taiwan, our plane lost an engine near Da Nang, but we turned back to Thailand, safely.

Several things, however, have caused me to think I should be more public with my support of Vietnam Veterans, and I decided to do so when I saw Joe and his ball cap.

Do you know…more than 200 Vietnam Veterans are dying daily? It'll soon be about 300. Do you remember?…the U. S. citizenry wasn't accepting of returning soldiers from Vietnam, the way we are now – thank God – of those from Iraq and Afghanistan. Returning to California back then, we eagerly changed into civilian clothes for the trip home, so someone wouldn't spit on us.

Do you realize how long I'd have been in prison by now if somebody had spit on me? I was no baby killer. I was just a young guy doing what I thought was my responsibility.

Do you know that more than 40,000 Vietnam Veterans have filed claims

for disabilities – cancer, etc. – from the effects of Agent Orange…and less than 1,000 have been compensated?

Do you know that many Vietnam vets still seek counseling for Post Traumatic Stress Disorder, PTSD? My friend Tommy, an Army draftee who crawled through the boonies, still has night sweats, nightmares, even though he did a "normal" career later as a railroad engineer. My friend Max in Santa Fe, a Special Forces soldier who worked with the Vietnamese Montagnards, "people of the mountains", still feels badly about our government abandoning them, even though he did a "normal" career later with the U. S. Geological Survey.

Both Max and Tommy continue to go for VA counseling.

You do know, don't you, that we'd have 58,000 more Vietnam Veterans if all those who got too close to those hornets had survived? Included are two special high school and college friends, Grant Stewart and Pete Moak.

So, for them, I've ordered my ball cap –Vietnam Veteran, U. S. Air Force – and await its momentary arrival. I'll first wear it on November 11th, to especially to honor "my" veterans of Vietnam, whether they lived or died.

May God bless the people who've served this country and the fine citizens who've supported them!

28

A Dark Christmas Story: The Secret War of Cowboy Bob and the Posse

December 2011

Sorry to do this, but here's a Scrooge-like story for your holiday consideration. I wouldn't have submitted it if it didn't seem important.

We know about current wars in Afghanistan and Iraq. Undoubtedly, certain government officials, including the President, receive daily casualty briefings.

But does anyone in national government give serious thought to another on-going battle here at home?

Since December 19, 2004, less than seven years… 1,121 persons have perished in this war. Unless something can be sensationalized, though, our liberal national news media isn't much interested even though more than 50% of victims have been killed by gunfire.

I'm talking about cops. When one dies, not many people outside his or her state even learn of it. Regarding Washington, D. C., the U. S.

Justice Department probably receives a report from the nearest FBI office. But then? Most likely, the notice is filed away unless there's some unusual publicity about the event.

If more than a thousand U. S. citizens had been killed in a foreign country in seven years, we'd likely have acted against that country.

My count starts on December 19, 2004, since Otero County Deputy Bob Hedman was killed on December 18th. Bob may be the first police officer you knew personally who died in the manner he did, and he may be one of the last you're aware of. Remember the trauma here in the aftermath? Multiply that times more than a thousand. And the beat goes on.

After Bob lost his life December 18, 2004, five more officers died that year. Three were killed on December 30th.

Police officer deaths nationwide have averaged 160 a year since. Calendar year 2007 was worst, when 200 officers met their end. Almost 21,000 police officers have perished violently in this nation's history.

But the numbers have greatly increased, starting in the 1970s, following the "peaceful" years after WWII.

This past October 22nd, I rested easily in my old '56 Shasta travel trailer at Stone Mountain, Georgia, while things went bump in the night outside. At the RV camp store, a poster promoted a fund raiser for the family of a Georgia officer who'd died not long before. Was it Willie Cammon, killed on March 3rd?...Buddy Christian, shot to death on March 22nd?...James Stewart, July 3rd?...or Derrick Whittle, September 18th? I don't recall.

While I slept, a bump occurred about five miles away, around 1:00 AM. Deputy Sheriff J. D. Paugh, protecting me, lost his life...shot at

30 times, hit nine times, by a National Guardsman with a rifle – domestic troubles – who then committed suicide.

On October 28[th], Officer Terry Mae Lewis-Fleming of the Albany, GA, Police Department died while pursuing robbery suspects. Detective Shane Wilson of the Doraville, GA, Police Department, was killed just days ago, November 14[th].

Georgia police officers are having a particularly tough year.

Likewise Florida, where 11 officers have died in 2011. Among them… Miami Detectives Roger Castillo and Amanda Haworth…in a shoot-out January 20[th]. Sgt Tom Baitinger and Officer Jeffrey Yaslowitz…by gunfire on January 24[th,] in St. Petersburg. And that same city mourned yet another officer…David Crawford, shot less than 30 days later.

During 2010, St. Petersburg's neighbor city, Tampa, lost Officers Jeffrey Kocab and David Curtis in a shootout on June 29[th].

Florida, the Land of Sunshine.

Since its formation, the San Antonio, Texas, Police Department , where I spent 23 years, has lost 51 officers. Six have been killed since December 2004. I knew four of them personally. Officer Stephanie Brown of the SAPD died on March 15[th] this year, struck by a drunk driver. Sgt Ken Vann of the Bexar County (San Antonio) Sheriff's Office died by gunfire on May 28[th].

Bob Hedman was the first Otero County deputy killed since Sheriff William Rutherford on February 13, 1923. Sheriff Rutherford, in office only six weeks, jumped on the running board of a car carrying escaped prisoners, who shot him with a stolen .30-.30 rifle. His killers were sentenced to death, but pardoned by the NM governor. Most likely an interesting political story.

Deputy Sheriff Bob Hedman's name engraved in the
Law Enforcement Memorial wall in Washington, DC.

I was visiting Mississippi this past October and learned that Captain John Haddock of the Grenada, MS, Police Department, had just died October 7th when intentionally struck by fleeing suspects in a vehicle doing 100 MPH.

Although originally from New York, Bob Hedman was a real cowboy. So forgive me if I think of him and his fellow officers who've given their all as members of the same posse. I visit his family annually, and just returned from New York State. I took your good wishes along. They're doing well, considering.

While there, I spoke by phone with the father of Bernalillo County (NM) Deputy Sheriff James McGrane, Jr., shot and killed in Albuquerque on March 22, 2006. Jim McGrane was 38. His parents stay busy raising funds for Officer Street Survival Training for NM policemen who wouldn't otherwise receive it.

Mr. and Mrs. McGrane have been cursed, flipped off, jeered at. But I know YOU are part of the more than 80% who will support their work. Donations are appreciated through their web site, www.deputymcgrane.com.

During the visit with Bob's family, I learned that Deputy Sheriff Kurt Wyman of the nearby Oneida County (NY) Sheriff's Office lost his life this past June 7th, by gunfire.

And while I wrote this dark article, Officer James Capoot of the Vallejo (CA) Police Department died on November 17th, shot by a bank robbery suspect. He was 43, a Marine Corps veteran survived by his wife and three daughters. Source of my data is the Officer Down Memorial Page, www.odmp.org.

Well…any hope out there for the Scrooges of our society? Any relief from the discontent, drugs, violence, lack of family unity that likely are causative factors of senseless violence? Where's The Ghost of Christmas Yet To Come when we need him?

Is it possible the real answer lies in the season at hand, the celebration of the birth of a Savior we should seriously pay attention to? Maybe Tiny Tim had it right, after all, when he so famously said:

"God bless us, everyone!" But I think we have to ask.

Author's Note: Update, September 10, 2015. The assault on American police officers continues. Since Officer James Capoot's death during 2011, another 577 have been killed in the line of duty. Altogether there were 180 deaths during 2011, a record year. To date, 83 have perished in 2015, including Officer Greg Benner of the Rio Rancho, New Mexico, Police Department, on May 25th. The most recent death is that of Lt.

FIFTY-SEVEN PIECES OF THE CLOUDCROFT PUZZLE

*Charles "GI Joe" Gliniewicz of the Fox Lake, Illinois, Police Department, September 1*st*. As of this writing, three suspects are at large in his murder. This number of deaths is unacceptable in a civilized society. Rest in peace, my brothers and sisters.*

29

Cloudcroft Love, Like an Old-Fashioned Phone Call

January 2012

Local Locals, those born here, will fight you over love of this village. Self-anointed Locals, those of us who've lived here full time some indeterminate number of years, also have a deep-seated passion for Cloudcroft. Those in between, who own a home and live here part time, can also be fanatics.

There's a fourth category, those folks who visit regularly, but for reasons of job - family - other - cannot move here from far off, but just cannot stay away. If we had a Local Application file, they'd be at the top of the candidate list. I guess they're Wantabe Locals. So love for Cloudcroft is a bit like an old-fashioned phone call, isn't it? Local or long-distance.

San Antonio TX Police Officer Mike Young and his family - wife Jan, children Chris and Sarah - fell into that fourth bunch. Mike, a devoted family guy, took his family on vacation, to the beach and to the mountains, at least twice a year. We were their mountains. For nine years, they stayed in the same rental on Maple, a house with Automatic

Stoop, just a couple of blocks from my place on Chautauqua Canyon. For that many years, I'd hear them unannounced in my driveway. Beep beep! Looking out, I'd see their beige Suburban. Happy days!

The kids grew up, and while doing so brought their girlfriend, their boyfriend, here...now those are wife and husband, respectively. Now there are grandkids. Other relatives came along. Everyone liked to play in the snow.

In 1979, Mike was at work in a patrol car, had the description of a robber. He stopped a young man on a bicycle, an unlikely mode of travel for such a suspect. Mike put his left hand up in desperation as the young man suddenly pulled a handgun and fired. The shot blew away Mike's left index finger. The robber fled to a downtown house nearby, almost in the shadow of the Tower of the Americas, if you've been there.

The perpetrator was killed, but not before two other officers were shot, one in the face with double aught buckshot from a 12 gauge shotgun. Miraculously, Sgt Coy Boone lived, as did the other officer. The entry to the house was haphazard, and the incident heralded the development of a modern-day SWAT team for our city. I was in charge of that team for five years. Mike, a tactical trainer in our academy, taught street survival skills for that long or longer. Having seen the elephant up close and personal, he did it well.

Both of us filed something away from that 1979 shooting. Mike: A lack of trust in humankind and maybe especially bicycle riders that according to Jan took him years to regain. Me: A knowledge that being shot in the head at close range doesn't necessarily mean being killed. Coy Boone took two years to recover, but he came back to work. As a matter of fact, Coy came to New Mexico to buoy me up in an Alamogordo courtroom in 2005, and he testified there. He had ridden with me on my rounds here as a deputy. He and his wife are frequent visitors to Cloudcroft RV parks.

Mike Young's career, and mine, paralleled in other ways. Leaving my five year assignment as a police helicopter pilot, Mike was my replacement. At 6'5", he was some replacement, filling way more than my shoes for seven years. Between us, we kept a seat warm for a third of that unit's history to date. At 6'5", Mike was too tall by military standards for pilots, both in total height and sitting height. And our little choppers didn't have adjustable seats. It was one size fits all.

So my vision of Mike Young was like that of Gunsmoke's Marshall Dillon, also one tall fellow, getting off a horse and into a Volkswagen. Our helicopters had rounded canopies. Mike looked like a backwards capital C getting inside a capital O. But he did the job and did it well, even folded over.

San Antonio, Texas, Police Officer Mike Young, always a long distance lover of Cloudcroft!

In 2005, both Mike and I received bad news, although of a different nature. Mike was diagnosed with cancer. But he was one of the most caring people I've ever known and he encouraged me beyond belief, in spite of his own troubles. Because of his own shooting, he truly understood.

"We're brothers, Billy, brothers in blue. Hang in there," he'd write me, while he dealt with his illness. Can you imagine? My problems were temporary, we all prayed his were. His family's visits to Cloudcroft, to the house on Maple with Automatic Stoop, stopped. No more beep beep, and I missed that.

Automatic Stoop? All really tall guys have that built in. They, perhaps unconsciously but automatically, bend over a little approaching door-ways, light fixtures. Of course, it was most evident in Mike when approaching helicopter rotor blades.

Mike fought the good fight the last six years. Bone marrow transplants, chemo, radiation. He felt bad last week and had to be taken to the emergency room. But picture this. Before leaving the house, Mike Young folded the laundry for Jan, straightened up his mother-in-law's room. Regrettably, he didn't return to his earthly home, passing away on December 13th. But of all the men I've known and I mean MEN, I believe Mike Young reached his heavenly home on December 13, 2011, and stood before his Savior, beaming!

The pastor said it well. Mike died too young but he achieved all his dreams. He had a beautiful wife, with rock-hard, solid love between them. He had beautiful children and grandchildren. He had an exciting job that most people would envy. If you don't believe that, you should have been at the grave site when the Schweitzer 333 turbine helicopter came blasting over at treetop level in a final salute. The pastor remarked that of all man's dreams, one isn't of growing old and feeble, and Mike didn't do that.

A year ago on December 16th, friend Smitty and I were bouncing about on a sailboat in 12 to 15 foot waves across the Gulf of Mexico, en route to Texas from Florida. If Mike hadn't been sick then, he may have been with us. We'd had lunch with him shortly before the trip.

December 16th, 2011, found Smitty and me bouncing on 20 foot waves of emotion as we did our best to provide a portion of Mike's eulogy. We were humbled to be asked to describe some part of this man's honorable life, and what he'd meant to us. Among what I said was that Cloudcroft, New Mexico, had missed Mike and his family the last six years.

Also among what I said to Jan and Cris and Sarah and their families was that the house on Maple is still there when they feel they're able to come back. It's a warm and welcoming place and we even left the Automatic Stoop on if anyone needs it.

Long-distance love, after all, like that old-fashioned phone call, works both directions.

30

For Valentine's Day, Everything You Wanted to Know about True Love in Cloudcroft, and ...

February 2012

Valentine's Day, a time to celebrate True Love! Having written previously about love OF Cloudcroft, here's some hints about finding love IN Cloudcroft. If you're looking, these tips will save you trouble and money.

Like a Hollywood movie, this may not be 100% true, but it is based on real stories.

Don't' worry. It's wintertime, and the oath I took as a peace officer - to protect life and property - extends to protecting you and your stuff from being thrown out of your house while it's cold, so your secrets are safe. Was that a collective sigh???

If now single, though, avoid hooking up just before January and February. This warning may extend to December through Easter, by which time the last snow has fallen.

Behavior during those time frames is often artificially better. Like a first date that lasts for months. No one wants to dig frozen clothes out of the snow, and spend the winter in a car or tent. Once I rescued my clothes from Texas mud, and that was bad enough, but at least they weren't stiff, the creases didn't cut. Here, beware of changing behavior after Easter. Remember, as the weather thaws, so may a personality frozen inside.

If someone will voluntarily snovel your show, or clear your frozen windshield, very good things. (Just seeing if you're paying attention. That's shovel your snow.)

Here are other useful winter hints. If he's a snow plow operator and doesn't berm up your driveway, it might indicate interest. (He equally means she.)

If he wants to secretly meet you on a snowy trail at a rendezvous he calls Old Place, maybe he's been there before? If he's a bird lover and says he recognizes the tracks of a Yellow Bellied Mattress Thrasher on the trail, run! Above all, avoid a rendezvous at Conception Point. Officially, no such place.

The best snow hint? Will he venture into a secluded canyon on a cold, miserable day and find you a blue spruce for a Christmas tree? Okay! But if you have to saw and drag? Well…

How about carving your initials into aspen trees? Let's say his name is Dirty Rat. No reason in itself to be suspicious, but look nearby at other trees. If you see many hearts with A. B. (AnyBody) + D. R., be cautious. Remember, too, that aspen is soft, easy to carve. Might indicate laziness. Seek out hardwood carvers instead.

Does he own anything? After all, money matters are the #1 cause of breakups…. Here's one. If he says he has his own propane wall heater, remember the fire may go out above 5,000 feet, and that doesn't necessarily mean on the heater.

What does he drive? Judge potential love candidates in this order (highest to lowest): AllWheelDrive/4WD… 4WD with manual hubs, he may want YOU to get out and turn the hubs… Front Wheel Drive only… 2WD pickups with rear wheel drive, spiked rear tires, weight in back...are you the weight?… 2WD pickups with chains, you may have to put on or help put on the chains. Hoh boy!… A "wood truck"? That's the last stop before the recycling plant.

Some special cases. Does he own a 2WD van? Worse than a 2WD pickup. Or, horrors, a boat? Double horror, a sailboat? Big red flag. To a sailor, Cloudcroft may be just another port in the storm.

Wants to borrow/use your vehicle? Kiss it - and him - goodbye and dial 1-800-SHERIFF.

Does he have a job? Be especially wary of handymen, real estate sales-men, deputy sheriffs. Handymen and real estate salesmen have seasonal incomes, not good. May leave for the Texas coast during wintertime. Handymen? One would think a licensed handyman, who plays by the rules, would be best. Not so. State restrictions are severe as to the work handymen can legally do, and the really smart ones don't get licenses. (I had a license.)

Deputy sheriffs have low salaries, although they do possess county gas cards, strictly for official use, of course, and their sheriffy trucks are nice 4WD pickups. Oh, and no manual hubs.

If he's a wood cutter and you paid for pine, but he delivered juniper, might be a keeper. Further, if he stacked the juniper (or even the pine), and you didn't pay extra, a plus. If you received this note: "Thanks for the business. You are nicely stacked…", signed - Hatchet Man - pro-ceed at your own risk. But if all that happened…the little hairs on the back of your neck stood up… AND you got an honest, full cord? Head straight for the church.

Are you an animal lover, seeking an animal lover? Avoid guys whose friends tease him this way: "Okay, I understand, but she's the ugliest elk in the village." Watch out for a woman who has 17 cats, a magic number.

Health issues? Dodge anyone who's allergic to houseflies or Miller Moths. Avoid persons with color blindness, too many double yellow lines here. Has back pain, needs oxycodone? Run like the wind. Is insurance coverage important? Do your flirting at the school, a bank or OCEC. Criminal background significant? Look up the FBI 10 Most Wanted list (#8 once turned up on a sheep ranch near Timberon), and on-line sexual predator lists. We've had our share.

Never, ever date a retired NASA rocket scientist. Why? C'mon, it's not rocket science.

Those arriving from other states often shed information at the state line. Number of prior marriages, teenage children, even wives. Be wary of those having arrived at the depot with lots of baggage. We have a depot but the train stopped running in 1947.

Ahhh! Love in Cloudcroft! A great place but with a limited number of potential single partners. The old saw here? There are so few eligibles around, when you leave town temporarily, you don't lose your Significant Other, just your turn.

God is great, of course, and the very best place to find someone special may be at church. Pew Love. Just be aware there is a variety of sheet fanner here referred to as a Pepe le Pew lover. Don't' confuse the two.

Well, good luck, and whatever, Happy Valentine's Day! Oh, the complete title of this story? "Everything You Wanted to Know about True Love in Cloudcroft, and Were Afraid I'd Write About…"

31

There's a Small New Star in the Western Sky

March 2012

"I shot the sheriff, but I did not shoot the deputy," sang rocker Eric Clapton in the 1960s, and before him Bob Marley.

"Shoot low, Sheriff, he's riding a Shetland," we joke to the man with the star, who's used to aiming at a desperado astride a taller horse.

The word goes around…"There's a new sheriff in town!" when one is elected, at which time the rules sort of change.

We sing and talk about our local sheriff like no other law enforcement official. We have a relationship to him that heads of other police agencies don't enjoy, and why is that? Because we directly control who occupies that office through the election process.

An elected sheriff should think and act like he's the top representative of law enforcement in his county, since he most closely represents the people who chose him.

One such guy who thought that way died suddenly on January 28, 2012. Johnny Lee, only 59, was your sheriff for 10 years, from 1993 through 2002. He ran for reelection in 2010, losing in the primary. While campaigning then, he was quoted this way:

"I had the honor of being elected for three straight terms," Lee said. "It's something no one has ever done. It's a faith and trust that I don't take lightly. I pinned my first law enforcement badge on 33 years ago. I am not ready to quit. I love it. I am a cop. This is my home. I was born and raised in Otero County. I want it to be the safest place."

Johnny Lee meant what he said.

During late 1996, I applied for the Otero County Sheriff's Office while still employed by the San Antonio TX Police Department, one of the largest agencies in the United States. I applied for a deputy's job for which I wasn't certified in New Mexico, just to meet Sheriff Lee and his staff. He told me to come back when I had my certification, so I paid my way through the police academy in Santa Fe and watched for openings, meanwhile going to work in Ruidoso Downs.

When I'd met him, he struck me as an old time Western sheriff, one of the last of a breed, it seemed. I liked his common sense approach and the way he thoughtfully pushed his cowboy hat back on his head when he talked. I appreciated, too, his service in Vietnam as a United States Marine.

The day I was hired, I drove to Sheriff Lee's office in Alamogordo. He ran out to meet me on the parking lot, a badge in hand, me in civilian clothes. "Raise your right hand. Do you swear to uphold the laws of New Mexico and Otero County, etc.?" he asked, tossing the badge my direction, giving me an address in Alamorosa. "Go out there and handle the call. We're short on deputies." So much for formality.

Former Sheriff Johnny Lee on duty in Zenith Park, Cloudcroft, 2006.

If a citizen wanted to discuss something with him, all they had to do was go by his office and knock. He had a true open door policy.

Johnny Lee never told us when to write or not write tickets, or when to make an arrest. "Use good judgment," he'd say, and he didn't interfere.

Johnny stood up for you, the citizens. When federal law enforcement agencies raided Moore's Trading Post at the bottom of the hill a few

years ago, without notifying him beforehand, he wasn't a happy camper and he told the feds so.

Term limits caught up with him in 2002 but he was short of paid-in time for retirement. Would the new sheriff, John Blansett, hire him as a deputy? It has to be strange to head an agency for a decade then again work at the entry level.

If you think a police agency isn't political, you've never worked at one. And sheriff's offices are the worst. Most deputies have an idea of one day becoming the sheriff. So a lot of hatchets are thrown around. For the most part, Sheriff John Blansett and ex-Sheriff Johnny Lee managed to bury their hatchets without burying them in each other.

Johnny came to work in the mountain district, and in a strange twist, I was suddenly his supervisor. I assigned him to the other shift as the senior officer. He handled it all with characteristic style and grace, and was someone you and I could depend on.

Enter December 18, 2004, the shooting I was involved in. I was dropped off at my house, alone, after being up all night. And what a night it had been. A certain deputy came by to check on me, to sit and spend time with me. When I revisited the scene later, a certain deputy went along. That same person would call frequently and see how I was. During my prison stay, that same guy wrote monthly, giving me the departmental gossip, keeping me in the loop, wishing me well.

When I returned from Santa Fe, a certain deputy was present to make sure I was still okay. That person, as you might guess, was Johnny Lee. Of course others helped a lot, but Johnny was always there.

He retired from the Otero County Sheriff's Office and began working at Alamogordo's Desert Lakes Golf Course. Golf, I think, was his third great love in life, behind wife Kay and being your sheriff. After his loss

in the 2010 primary, I drove to Desert Lakes to once again tell him how much I appreciated him and honestly, to console him a little.

He was out mowing fairways and I waited until he rode in on a tractor. Every candidate for office who's run before has a garage full of political signs. "Will you run again, Johnny?" I asked. "I've put the signs away, Billy," he said, pushing his cowboy hat back as usual, in a contemplative way, while we sat and talked. "They won't be coming back out."

I'm not sure that was true. Regrettably, though, he was right. But you and I were fortunate to have had Sheriff John Alan Lee in office for 10 years, and I was lucky to have known him and worked for him. He was a darned fine boss and a good cop. May God bless his family, may he rest in peace.

32

The Day of the Broom

April 2012

Cloudcroft, home of… Beautiful sunsets. Dumpster diving. Fast drivers who pass on double yellows. Love. An Outhouse race (not to be confused with Love). Tolerable and intolerable karaoke. Good cheeseburgers. One Pittsburgh Steelers fan. The last VW bus in America. Ghosts, a laundromat, three Democrats, one philosopher, and much, much more!

It's an extensive list, but something has been missing. We've never directed a major international scientific study. Recently, though, the CCC - Cloudcroft Control Center - was activated to conduct the IBE…International Broom Experiment. Seriously!

You see, as this is written, on March 20th, the Infernal - oops, that's Vernal - Equinox is on us. Precisely at 5:14 AM today, the sun was perfectly balanced over the equator, with sunrise everywhere in the world occurring precisely at 6:00 AM, sunset exactly at 6:00 PM.

Vernal Equinox? Here's a Wikipedia definition: "An equinox happens each year at two specific moments in time, when there is a location (the subsolar point) on the Earth's equator, where the center of the Sun can

be observed to be vertically overhead, occurring around March 20[th] and September 22nd each year."

Okay, we LOCALS understand that, but how can Cloudcroftians demonstrate this to the world, so that simpler folk everywhere also comprehend? Well, by doing just this: Standing our brooms up! During the Vernal Equinox, a broom will stand by itself, unflinching, at attention, very easily. With some care and patience, even an egg will do so. And to prove it works everywhere, the CCC initiated a study March 10, 2012. Hey, is this cool, or what?

That day, electronic notification - okay, e-mails - flashed across the United States, yes, around the globe, from Cloudcroft, New Mexico, with this charge: Gentlemen (and Ladies), Stand Your Brooms! (Eggs were mentioned, though not with the same fervor...) Note, please, this will work days BEFORE and AFTER the Equinox, since the sun is so nearly centered leading up to and following the exact time...it's not too late to try it.

Sure, there are skeptics, but I sure didn't expect them in OUR little corner of the world. Maybe you've seen a billboard on the outskirts of Alamogordo, coming up from El Paso, said billboard with a pronouncement at its bottom: "Say the word 'GULLIBLE' very, very slowly, and it sounds like 'ORANGE'."

Al, a local Cloudcroft intellect and the last person I expected to skeptacise, responded with that exact phrase. (I've said it very slowly, by the way - G U L - L I - B L E - and it does NOT sound like ORANGE.) So scratch Big Al from the list of participants. Wow, just because a serious study is to be published April 1[st]...

Others, though, responded enthusiastically! From across the United States, here were some candid replies: (in the interest of science, no punches are pulled)...

From Jerry in Ft. Myers, Florida: "You really need to get a life."

Harrumph. Never liked him much anyway. He's been jealous of me since I was voted Most Handsome in high school.

Up a bit to Ocala, Florida, and Louise, her response accompanied by a photo of a corn broom and a whisk broom standing side by side: "Yes! Here are our brooms - mother and baby. Billy, you are a genius!" Now that was more like it! I really like this lady...

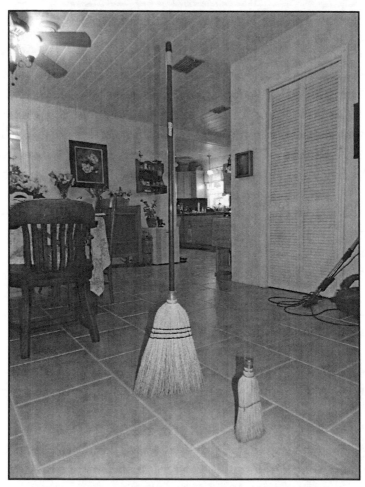

These mother and child brooms proudly stand tall in Florida during the Vernal Equinox of 2012.

Way up to New York State, from Jackie: "As you asked, drove the short distance to the American side of Niagara Falls, and stood my broom on the sidewalk. But it fell into the river, and was swept over the falls." No picture was included. Her broom, SWEPT over the falls? Sure it was. I'm trying to remember how to spell "Gul-li-ble".

On to Jere in Tennessee: "Actually, the REAL question would be to find the first person to actually fly off on one of those stand-alone brooms. I do have a next-door neighbor I could volunteer for you. She fits the profile quite nicely!" Oh boy. Seems like a Jere is a Jerry, no matter how you spell it, doesn't it?

From Bob, in Nashville, Tennessee: "BILLY, THERE'S BROOMS EVERYWHERE! - BOB" (What do you mean, EVERYWHERE?), I wrote back...) "I MEAN THEY'RE STANDING EVERYWHERE! - BOB" You begin to get a sense of the pace of life in Tennessee, don't you? No photo, though.

To Mississippi, and Brenda in her hair saloon: "Here's a picture of my broom, standing tall and proud, but I refuse to be shown with it. A lot of the people in this town think I'm a witch anyway, and this would be visual proof they're right." Hmmm? Does she own a vacation home in Tennessee, next door to Jere?

Over to Texas, where Debbie does Dallas: "I felt very silly trying this, but your e-mail looked legit. Here's a photo of our garage broom standing next to our toilet plunger. It works!" I was happy to get her response but everyone knows that a toilet plunger works. I guess even a broom needs a friend, though.

Down to San Antonio, Texas, to Frances: "Hi Billy. I have too much time on my hands, had to try your scientific experiment. Attached are pictures of the standing egg and broom. Oh...don't tell anyone but I graduated from Hogwarts School of Witchcraft and Wizardry... LOL!!!!!!!" Having heard from several Broomers, I cannot describe my

level of excitement on hearing from a successful Egger, and an obvious Harry Potter reader...

It took 10 minutes to coax the egg into standing, Frances said. I warned her the Equinox Police might come by to check for Super Glue on the egg's tip. (Her husband, Al, denied the Super Glue insinuation but confessed it might be Gorilla Glue. As he's their poster boy, he may have been serious.)

Yes, I said International study. Frank, my retired Liverpool, England, police officer friend, who now lives in Singapore, was our overseas participant. Ever since I obtained a Texas Ranger Stetson for him, he's acquiesced to my every whim, so I knew he'd cooperate. His response? "Billy, I'm in Hong Kong just now. In a hotel and don't have a broom or an egg. My Chinese customers will think I'm nuts if I ask for either one. LOL!" Okay, Frank, that's great, Laugh Out Loud if you like, but I want the darn Stetson back.

So...the CCC is quiet now, our brooms having stood the test, so to speak. Don't fear, this is something you CAN still do safely at home. Should you forget, though, remember...the Autumnal Equinox occurs September 22, 2012, and you can even sleep late and try it...the exact time will be 2:49 PM. Stand aside, Sunspot, we're coming through!

33

Linc'ing Up and Re-Joyce'ing With Friends in North Carolina

May 2012

Where in Cloudcroft does one go to see a friend, or a non-friend, for that matter? Burro Street? A bank or cafe? The library? Maybe. But the guaranteed location - and time - since the village doesn't have home mail delivery, is the Post Office lobby, at 10:00 AM, Monday thru Friday. It's a can't miss.

Two such folks I used to encounter there were Linc and Joyce Neal. But they succumbed to the demands of family and health, and headed east towards Virginia in the summer of 2002. They almost made it.

During 2006, while beset by troubles, I received a very supportive letter from Linc and Joyce, who now live in Brevard, North Carolina. In an empty brain slot in my head (there are many), I noted they were "over there" somewhere, and vowed that someday I'd visit and thank them personally.

Just last week, in Tennessee, visiting a very sick friend, that little brain

cell started flashing red. Was I close? Checking, it was just a few hours east. So I called, and yes, they'd be home. Fantastic!

We had a great half day together, me getting the nickel tour, us having lunch at the downtown Square Root restaurant. Were your ears burning? They should have been!

Hard to believe that the Neals have been gone a decade. They'd lived in El Paso for many years, as Linc worked at White Sands Missile Range as an engineering psychologist on U. S. Army programs. Joyce served as a speech therapist at the El Paso School for the Deaf.

In 1968, Gilbert Lincoln Neal and his wife Joyce did what El Paso folks have done for eons. They discovered Cloudcroft, with its cooler temperatures and beautiful mountain forests. Then they purchased a Twin Forks cabin for $3500. Some of their Texas friends bought vacation homes nearby.

Their only bathroom was outdoors, made from a packing crate to contain a belly tank for an Air Force F-100 fighter bomber. A very small stall...one could go in and come back out in only one direction. The Neals had two toddlers. The outhouse grossed out the children, whose G. O. meter pegged at 10 when they discovered a bat sleeping inside.

Linc carefully collected the bat and carried it to a remote woodpile. The bat just as carefully flew back and resumed its rightful place. Later, local resident Fred Griffin dug a septic tank hole - did they leave the outhouse for the bat?...I didn't ask - and many fossils were unearthed. Their children delighted in playing with the fossils.

An El Paso friend, a meticulous planner installing a new plumbing system in an adjoining cabin, was euphoric when he flushed the toilet the first time, and it worked. But before assembly, he'd left the parts out in view of his children. One had inserted a croquet ball into a pipe. On the third flush, the system exploded!

Linc retired from federal civil service in 1992, Joyce from the Texas teacher system. They moved to Cloudcroft fulltime, having built a home on Columbine during 1991. The Neals found out what fish diving into the local pool have discovered for years…it's not so important what you did before you got here, but what you do after you get here.

Linc Neal, though, is a get things done kind of guy. He was a Cloudcroft city councilman for four years, 1999 through 2002. During his term, he was instrumental in having the village assume responsibility for operation of the library. He served as Assistant City Magistrate for two years, and among the things he did there was marry folks.

Linc recalls a wedding in Zenith Park, during a warm February. The bride and groom were wearing shorts. A cold front suddenly moved through, quickly bringing snow and freezing temperatures. As Judge Neal was saying: "If there's anyone here who has an objection and wants to voice it…", the groom yelled out: "Can you hurry it up? It's getting mighty cold out here!"

The Neals remember many good friends…Judy Henry and Tom and Barbara Springer, with whom they worked on Rails to Trails; Jim and Betty Morrison, parents of Terri Scott; Fred and Judy Walters; Chuck and Joyce Komraus; Earl and Dixie Neill; Carolyn and Jerry Heinzelmann; and numerous others. Betty Morrison has visited them in North Carolina.

A favorite memory is of Terri Scott's dog Dooley. Dooley, they said, was bummed by the lack of attention after Terri and Tim Scott's first child was born, and was often rescued from dumpsters where he'd gone to sulk. Another time, while everyone fled, Dooley was spotted walking side by side down the street with a bear, seemingly desperate for friendship.

Joyce recalled the first time another bear came close to their home

on Columbine, her screaming for help from Linc, who was taking a shower. Her hero rushed to the rescue, buck naked, and the bear, for a reason only it might recall, ran away.

Joyce, 82, and Linc, 83, stay in touch with village activities through the Mountain Monthly. Linc said he'll only cancel his subscription "…when I don't recognize the name of anyone I know…or, when a certain party is elected to political office." In the interest of libel prevention, I declined his offer to name that party!

Joyce looked wistful as she said: "I'm so very glad we lived in Cloudcroft. It was a big part of our life." When moving eastward, she consciously looked for a place that reminded her of our area. "I had to have my mountains and my four seasons," she explained. Brevard is adjacent to the Appalachian Mountains, is in the Great Smoky Mountains, and adjoins the Pisgah National Forest. It's close to Asheville.

Peaks in the area go up to 6,000 feet, the land is lush and green, and there are lakes and rivers. It's very beautiful. Transylvania County is called the Land of Waterfalls. I hiked to several, including Triple Falls, featured in the current movie The Hunger Games. Nearby Lake Lure was used in the filming of the movie Dirty Dancing.

Linc and Joyce have now lived in North Carolina for 10 years, and their home is for sale. They're within a full day's drive of family in Virginia but want to get closer. Meanwhile they remain active in their community. They've helped raise funds for a beautiful new library, and Linc serves as a mediator for the courts.

They send greetings to Cloudcroft, and I took your good wishes to them. May God bless the Neals, good friends, as they keep on trucking!

Linc and Joyce Neal, former Sacramento Mountain residents,
at their home in Brevard, North Carolina.

34

The True Story of the Train That Saved a Space Shuttle

June 2012

At the Texas Pit BBQ café in Cloudcroft for many years, one could glance up to see an aging 8X10 black and white photograph of space shuttle Columbia landing at White Sands during 1982. A proud moment for New Mexicans, it was the only time an Orbiter landed here.

While having lunch at a deli in Mississippi recently, a fellow diner said he'd retired from NASA, so I mentioned the photograph to him. David Hoffman is his name, and he really perked up when I talked about that shuttle landing.

He was at White Sands that day, he explained, and said the successful touchdown was the culmination of the most hectic 72 hours in his life. "It was the only time a train may have saved a space shuttle," he stated. Curious, I asked him to elaborate.

After college graduation, Mr. Hoffman, a Florida native, went to work for a railroad. That job led to one with NASA and their giant

crawler-transporter tracked vehicles used to transport spacecraft from the assembly building to the launch complex. The pair of crawler-transporters are the largest self-powered land vehicles in the world.

A team of nearly 30 engineers, technicians and drivers operated the vehicles, nicknamed Hans and Franz. They weren't fast and they weren't economical. Traveling at 1 mph or less, they burned more than 125 gallons of diesel fuel per mile.

The March 1982 flight of shuttle Columbia was the third flight, STS-3. Then, officials felt that touching down on a "soft" lake bed was the only acceptable place since the aircraft's tires weren't engineered for hard surface runways. So the Edwards Air Force Base, California, dry lake bed was the primary landing site.

White Sands Space Harbor was second on the list. About 40 van loads of support gear were pre-positioned in California. NASA had spent a year preparing to move that equipment to New Mexico should conditions make such a choice necessary.

Giant Air Force C-5 cargo planes would be utilized but it would take time to make all the flights. Lots of time. Driving everything the 1000 miles between California and New Mexico was considered but rejected. A "just in case" backup plan to move things by railroad was developed.

All railroad buffs, be their focus the real trains or models, know the big yellow and red diesel locomotives of the Santa Fe Railway. That railroad served Edwards AFB and thus was the originating carrier for providing the railcars if needed to move them to El Paso, Texas.

Southern Pacific Railroad locomotives would then pull the train from El Paso to Alamogordo on their track, where Holloman AFB locomotives would move everything on government trackage to Holloman, next to White Sands. Air Force locomotives? Sounds funny, doesn't it? Using government tracks would ensure that primary rail lines weren't blocked.

To be ready, Santa Fe RR even took two 89 foot flatcars and modified them to carry two giant highway vans of specialized equipment, and kept them immediately available in California.

"RAIN! MORE RAIN!! LOTS MORE RAIN!!!" exclaimed David Hoffman, about the month of March 1982, before Columbia launched on March 22 nd. Edwards' dry lake bed was anything but. With compelling reasons to maintain the liftoff date, David was the only transportation person in the room at Kennedy Space Center when a decision was made to land in New Mexico.

"We're going to White Sands. Do you have a plan?" David was asked, with 72 hours to spare. "Yes, sir," he replied, and within six hours was on a non-stop flight to Los Angeles.

Mr. Hoffman said the next 48 hours were a blur, but - speaking of the Santa Fe line crews - "I've never worked with a nicer and more helpful group of people." Three spit and polish almost new 3,000 horsepower diesel locomotives, resplendent in their red and yellow colors, were there, with enough spare parts aboard to almost build a fourth. Supervisory personnel manned the crews, the train dubbed "The Space Shuttle Express" by network news helicopters constantly overhead.

The space shuttle program was an exciting topic then, to a nation ready for good news after the political debacle of the Vietnam War. The loading finished, the train roared eastward toward El Paso, the main lines held open, throttles open as wide as track speeds permitted. David flew to Texas to make sure Southern Pacific was ready. And they were. SP was happy to show off their skills and equipment for the run up to Alamogordo, but disappointed it happened at night.

Arriving in Alamo, David found that an Air Force locomotive relief crew, flown in at the last moment, wasn't familiar with the rails near Holloman AFB. His last 24 sleepless hours were spent in the cab with them, loading and unloading.

But it all came together. NASA honchos had been worried that critical equipment would be broken in the rush. The final tally, though - two broken glass dials, quickly repaired! With precious little time to spare, everything was finally in place, to prevent critical damage to the Orbiter.

Did you know?...Wikipedia reports that Columbia experienced autopilot problems during landing, with the touchdown one of the more dramatic of the program, the landing gear deploying at just 150 feet off the ground at 275 knots, locked into place just 5 seconds before landing. Ultimately, though, Columbia arrived safely!

So, yes, the shuttle could land in the desert, but sand - hey, c'mon, we know it's really gypsum, not sand - damaged the Orbiter, another reason White Sands dropped on the desired list of future landing places.

The decision to move support equipment by rail saved NASA $2 million in transportation costs. David Hoffman smiled as he finished his story. "So the ole Iron Horse beat the airplanes to the punch; saved taxpayers a bundle of money compared to the alternatives; and in my opinion, saved space shuttle Columbia by getting the support gear in place and protecting its critical equipment for future flights."

Very exciting, but finally time for the most important question. "Did you get up to Cloudcroft?" I asked. "Sorry, no ," he said, explaining he had to immediately return to Kennedy Space Center after making certain everything would be returned safely to California, again by train.

It was tough telling him that after all that work, he'd missed the best part.

35

"The Art of Racing in the Rain", a book review by Sara Lee

August 2012

Note: I mysteriously received this in the mail. Since I'm very busy this month and don't have time to write, we'll use this instead. Thanks! Billy Anders

My name is Sara Lee and I'm a dog. I weigh 50 pounds. I have big ears and I'm probably a hound. I came here four and a half years ago. I live with a Man and a Woman and my friend Yellow Dog in James Canyon.

I was just Sara but Billy who got me out of prison – yes, I have a criminal record - would hum a little tune: "Everybody doesn't like something, but nobody doesn't like Sara Lee!" So Sara Lee I became.

Watching television recently, Yellow and I heard a book being discussed. I was surprised to learn many of you don't know dogs think like people. Hey, we understand everything you say. We can't talk, though, for a good reason.

Our tongues don't waggle properly. They're long and thick and flappy. So the sounds we make seem strange to you. Like, if we see danger, we yell: "Watch out!" But you hear: "Bark!"

And, we don't have opposable thumbs. That's why, for instance, we lap up water, time consuming. If we had opposable thumbs, like humans, we'd each have a glass with our name on it so we wouldn't get germs. Sometimes I dream of tipping a glass up to my lips, drinking slowly and deeply, instead of lapping.

Guess what else has opposable thumbs? Monkeys. Please do not confuse me or Yellow with monkeys. They're stupid. I can't imagine wearing a little red suit, holding a money cup, and hanging around with an organ grinder. How degrading.

Like humans, we dogs start thinking about something else and get off the subject, like now. So back to the book. It's called" The Art of Racing in the Rain", by Garth Stein. If you'll read it, you'll understand your dog better. Miss Joyce at the little red building probably has it.

What's it all about, Alpo? (That's a joke.) There's this dog Enzo and a man named Denny. Denny wants to be a race car driver, so does Enzo. Denny meets Eve and Enzo is jealous but learns to love Eve. Eve has Zoe and Enzo is jealous but they become best friends. Oh, one thing about dogs is that we can smell. Oh boy can we! Our noses are about 40,000 times more sensitive than humans' noses. When we pass gas, for example, it's okay, but when people do it, it's rough, so take it outside, please.

Anyway Enzo early on is able to smell a deadly illness on Eve before she or Denny knows about it, but Enzo can't tell anyone, because he can't talk, remember? And he couldn't write a note. Again that doggone lack of opposable thumbs.

Enzo also explains that dogs don't go to heaven, they're reincarnated

as a human then get their chance the next time around. That becomes important in the book.

Denny got Enzo from a puppy farm. I remember when I was a puppy. I was a pretty strange duck once. Maybe you have a dog you got when it was older. Yellow is adopted, too, from a previous life but that's all I know. She hasn't told me because we can't talk, remember?

Yellow jumps in her sleep sometimes. Maybe she's dreaming about more than chasing a rabbit. But we're both very happy now.

My brothers and sisters and I were born at Puppy Prison #17. Later a rancher came for me. I never saw my mother or brothers or sisters again. I was sad but it happens to dogs that way. The rancher's name was Jolly and he was anything but. So quickly, I got a bad feeling about people. But without opposable thumbs, we need them to pull the string on the puppy chow sack, and turn the water faucet on.

Jolly wore cowboy boots with long skinny toes. He could kick a roach in a corner and kill it. He was impatient but hey, I was just a puppy. When I'd spill food, he'd throw the food bowl at me. Or kick me in the ribs. Ouch. We're strong but our ribs are vulnerable. If I was slow through a door, he'd slam me with it. Soon enough, I didn't trust food bowls, would rather just eat off the floor. "Dagnabbit, Sara, keep it in the bowl!" he'd yell.

I became fearful of feet, the human part that boots go on. The boots seemed harmless enough off those feet, but I didn't cozy up to them, just in case.

After two years, Jolly returned me to Puppy Prison and lied. "She's a calf chaser," he said, "can't keep her." Calf chaser my tail! We were just playing. Know how big calves get? They're the last thing you'd make mad on a ranch.

Then Billy paid my bail, got me out. I got a little tired of hearing about Cookie, his previous dog, she couldn't have been that cool. Anyway bet she didn't get kicked in the ribs. He seemed trustworthy, but I kept cautious. Then he started traveling a lot, and I stayed with Yellow Dog and the Man and Woman three times.

What a great place! After the third time, the Man asked Billy if I could live there. Billy said yes pretty fast to suit me, but I think he was sick that day, because his eyes were wet.

Here's what I wish, though. That Ole Jolly could see me now!

The Woman and Yellow and I take a three mile walk in the forest every day. Sometimes, during that walk (and dogs do this) we revert to impulsive "dog" behavior. It's just built in. Once, I did that and chased a squirrel that had arrows on its head. At the vet's office, they called that squirrel a porcupine. Ouch. Live and learn. Porcupines, like monkeys, by the way, are stupid.

Yellow and I have great food and nobody there wears boots, and feet behave themselves. The bowls sit still and I trust them and feet and even doors nearly 100%. I'm allowed to go through doors at my own pace. Life is so great! Yes, there's even room in this world for a dog falsely accused of crime. Chasing calves? Pardon me, not true.

Well, again I strayed off the book, but I hope you'll read it. Remember, it's called "The Art of Racing in the Rain". Have a tail-wagging great day! Your friend (now), Sara Lee

Sara Lee, book reviewer, sitting patiently on Columbine in Cloudcroft, 2008.

36

Welcome to the Mountains!
Snow Driving 101...

October 2012

New to the Sacramentos? Soon the snow will fly, and Cloudcroft will be beautiful with a winter wonderland look, and you're gonna be driving in it.

If you're a flatlander who's never driven in snow, you're in for some fun.

As flatlanders ourselves, my wife and I first visited Cloudcroft during December 1993, staying at the Silvertop Cabins for a week. They're now The Cabins @ Cloudcroft. Six inches of snow fell, and it was unexpected.

The gorgeous, peaceful snowfall was a major reason we decided to move here and did so three years later.

Our learning experience began quickly. We had a two wheel drive car, a Honda Accord. Access to the cabins was downhill from Coyote, or uphill from Grand. A'slipping and a'sliding. An eye-opener, but luckily we departed accident free.

Before our permanent move during Thanksgiving 1996, a 1986 Ford Bronco was acquired. It was our first 4WD vehicle, and had manual front hubs that required one to get out and twist the knob on each front wheel to engage 4WD.

Arriving at the Burro Street Boarding House, I turned the Bronco off Burro Avenue onto the steep little snow covered street. I was towing a small loaded trailer, it was cold, I was tired. My first mistake - to attempt the short climb in 2WD. The truck slid backwards and I very nearly jackknifed, but was able to get out and twist the hubs, and regain momentum.

My welcoming committee had very nearly been a one man affair. Joe Mancillas of Cloudcroft Wrecker.

Lesson One, learned quickly, was that having 4WD is desirable. Lesson Two, engage it before you actually need it. More discoveries followed, including some made in personal vehicles, and more in a sheriff's pickup across more than seven years of scooting about in some of the worst winter weather.

My boss, Sgt Jeff Farmer, a local, emphasized the following. Keeping your speed at 50 mph or less in all conditions, most definitely to include snow, gives you time to react to animals and may prevent careening on black (invisible) ice. When on a gravel road, slower speed keeps rocks from blowing out your tires. Thanks to Jeff's good advice, I never hit an animal or blew out a tire.

I'd already had an adventure on black ice, near Mescalero, on Highway 70. It happened in my personal Jeep Cherokee with 4WD, en route to my previous job with the Ruidoso Downs Police Department. I'd bought the Jeep in Dallas TX. The tires, with 80% tread, showed no weather cracking. Lesson learned: Tires that have been used in extreme heat may look great but have developed a very hard surface. If so, they'll slip very easily.

I became a believer shortly afterwards, returning to Cloudcroft from Ruidoso at only 30 mph in snow. Driving in 2WD on a straightaway in almost a level place, the Jeep suddenly reversed directions, went over an embankment, and down about 10 feet. Luckily, 4WD got me out. New (softer) Goodyear Wranglers were purchased the next day.

Many believe bigger wider tires are better in snow. Jeff explained the exact opposite is true. A wide tire forces up a layer of snow and pushes it ahead, while a slim size cuts through, maintaining traction.

In these tough times, 10% or more of tire sales nationally are used tires. Caution…weather cracking is common in our drier climate, and tires deteriorate from the inside, too. All tires made since 2000 have a four digit number code in a little box on the sidewall. Usually it isn't wise to buy a tire more than two years old. A tire with the number code 4607, for example, was manufactured in the 46th week of 2007. Don't go there.

Here's a "Mountain Rule", a necessary thing to master during Honorary Local qualification. When two vehicles meet on an icy/snowy/slick narrow road, you as the downhill driver should yield, give way. Maintenance of momentum is critical for the person traveling up-hill. Not observing this tradition will identify you as a rookie quicker than an auto burglar alarm.

Going down the mountain to Alamogordo in the wintertime? Check the weather forecast first. When the snow flies, a return trip uphill will be more difficult, maybe almost impossible. If you try it in a 2WD rear wheel pickup or van, every deputy already knows in advance where you'll come to a stop. Just above Bailey Canyon is one place. Other roads like Highway 244 also have their magical lack-of-forward progress points.

Important. If it suddenly starts snowing and you decide to get out of Dodge immediately to "beat the weather", don't. Be patient, avoid

panic. Within two hours, the snowplows and sand trucks will be operating and you won't already be in the ditch east of town, in the curve just before the ski area.

US Highway 82, near the ski area just east of Cloudcroft on a snowy day when patience is a virtue.

Using common sense, even a 2WD pickup will get you through wintertime. The old timers had nothing else. My 1993 GMC pickup, with sandbags in the back, snow tires on the rear, chains for real emergencies (never used them), and a tow strap in the tool box (did use it), did so for five years. Carry your own tow strap, by the way. Always. A snow shovel is a good idea, too.

Be at peace with Berm Law: "Shovel the berm away…but thanks to the snowplow…it's back the next day." Know that a berm ignored melts during the day but refreezes at night, and quickly becomes an icy obstacle that can block access indefinitely.

Fresh snow? Make a new track when possible, better traction. Preplan

not only getting where you're going, but your eventual departure from there, your vehicle facing forward and downhill if you can.

Blizzards? Get them at a Dairy Queen, not on Highway 82. If heavy, blowing snow persists, find a motel room. I've spent the night at Holloman AFB rather than try to drive up the hill.

Remember, you came to Cloudcroft for the relaxed life style, to leave hurry and worry behind. A beautiful snowfall is peaceful and serene, best enjoyed with hot apple cider, hot chocolate or coffee, not anxiety.

Thank God for your blessings, breathe deeply and enjoy. After all, you're living in a place that other people come to on vacation.

Use 4WD to get yourself out of trouble, not into it, and don't forget that tow strap!

37

A Cloudcroft Christmas is a Very Good Thing

December 2012

In a world beset by economic and political uncertainty, there are a few very good things left. One of them is a Cloudcroft Christmas.

A Christmas in Cloudcroft may be in your own home, a rental cabin, or at The Lodge or Cloudcroft Hotel. Regardless of where you stay, it's about having your family with you.

Your meals may be home-cooked or eaten at Rebecca's or at the Western or Dave's or some combination of those and more. They might be chicken-fried steak or enchiladas or cheeseburgers, or something fancier.

Your dessert could well be a fresh hot pie from the Mercantile. Ummm good! You may have a drink at the Western or The Lodge. Not for intoxication, just for relaxation. A Cloudcroft Christmas can help you relax, leave stress behind.

FIFTY-SEVEN PIECES OF THE CLOUDCROFT PUZZLE

An essential, your Christmas tree, may be one already decorated for you; an old favorite kept in a dusty box; or a real tree. The latter come in two varieties: from the Allsup's lot, or better yet, straight from the Lincoln National Forest, after having obtained the $5 permit.

If you harvested your own tree, it probably came from a secret place where the good ones grow. You hiked there, cut the tree with a tinge of sadness but knowing how much happiness it would bring. You may have dragged it back to the car a distance, maybe through some snow.

Decorating your own tree makes Christmas all the better, especially if your children help, whether they're still little or even fully grown.

If you stay in a rental cabin, it may be in a place where cell phone reception isn't good. Not to worry. You'll have an old TV with a DVR or even a VHS player and you'll watch old movies. Or open a drawer and find something almost unusual now. Books. Or even board games. Amazing to play Monopoly or Scrabble again with your family, isn't it? Amazingly good, to reconnect.

The texting, twittering and Facebooking can wait, for once. Face to face is better anyway.

Need that last minute perfect gift? There's casual shopping on Burro Street, on the boardwalk.

And how about that hiking? On the OSHA trail or others, up and down steep paths, careful where there's ice or snow. To old places long familiar, new places never seen. Going slowly, of course, because of the altitude, but breathing in the sharp, fresh mountain air. Unmatched at lower levels.

I've traveled more this year, and regret that my last view of Cloudcroft was in the rear view mirror. Last month found me in Winter Harbor, Maine, a small Cloudcroft-size New England fishing village on the

Atlantic coast. Lobsters are a big deal there. Like Cloudcroft, Winter Harbor is a picture-perfect location for a postcard. The fall colors were out in force.

Anyone remember Norman Rockwell Christmas covers on the Saturday Evening Post? It was fun to visit the Rockwell museum in Stockbridge, Massachusetts. The entire trip was one of adventure and misadventure. A big truck rattled my room in another Massachusetts town. The next day I learned the truck had been a 4.5 earthquake, centered 20 miles away. Ignorance is truly bliss, isn't it?

After 30 plus years of driving police cars, sometimes at 100 mph or more, without a serious accident: I was T-boned by two Russians speeding in a German car, within sight of Ft. William Henry. The fort is at the southern end of Lake George, in the Adirondacks of New York. Historically important during the French & Indian Wars, it's featured in James Fennimore Cooper's book, "The Last of the Mohicans".

One of God's blessings, though: A totaled car but no serious injury. Back on the road with a replacement rental the next day.

Deputy Bob Hedman's mother and brothers were doing well in upper New York State and sent their greetings. I reminded them that you remember, even after eight years.

Travel is great fun but honestly, I'll miss my Cloudcroft Christmas, won't get out the old yellow bow saw to trek to You-Don't-Know-Where Canyon for a tree. Don't feel too sorry for me, though.

Christmas 2012 will be unusual. A tough job, but someone has to do it. A friend in Hawaii needs a house-sitter for the holidays, someone to feed Maca the cat. My wife and I were pretty quick to volunteer. The tough part? Maca has claws. She's down to eight lives, incidentally. The home is a 9th floor condo in downtown Honolulu and Maca recently

fell off the balcony railing. Luckily, to an obstruction only 30 feet below on the 7th floor where she landed safely.

Word is the refrigerator is stocked and the car is full of gasoline. Boogie boarding at the beach will be a strange replacement for Cloudcroft hiking or snow play, but such opportunity doesn't knock that often.

In spite of this Hawaiian adventure, I'm envious of your Cloudcroft Christmas and look forward to seeing the village in the windshield ahead, not in the rear view mirror. Happy Holidays to each of you!

You're appreciated for what you mean to me, and I don't forget that. Oh, drop into a Cloudcroft church for a Christmas service and a reminder of what the season is all about, will you? That's one of the few other good things left. Aloha!

38

Happy New Year! Looking Back to Look at the Future

January 2013

Sometimes, greeting a New Year, it's good to look at historical events that ultimately guaranteed a good future for Americans. In December's paper, I mentioned my good fortune in being able to visit Hawaii during the Christmas holidays. Luckily, my time there coincided with the 71st anniversary of the attack on Pearl Harbor, and I couldn't resist the opportunity to attend the ceremony.

As expected, high ranking officials presided and they said the right things. Hawaiian trade winds blew briskly and U. S. flags popped and snapped, looking great. It was good to see but I knew that survivors of the attack would be in attendance. About 30 were. Thus my real goal was to meet some of them, shake their hands, and tell them "thank you" on behalf of you, our Mountain Monthly readers. I wanted to ask what they remember most about that fateful day.

Mr. Robert P. Irwin of Cameron Park, California, and Mr. Ewalt Schatz of Moreno Valley, California, were both 18 year old Navy men

who survived the attack, on separate ships. They've known each other in later years from having been neighbors in Cameron Park where Mr. Schatz also formerly lived, and were sitting together this year. I'll save you the math, and mention that each is now 89. They graciously allowed me to join them after the speeches.

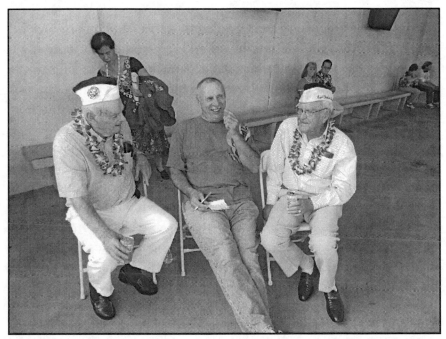

Seventy-one years later, Robert Irwin, left, and Ewalt Schatz, right, Pearl Harbor survivors, tell me about December 7, 1941.

According to Wikipedia, the battleship USS Pennsylvania was in dry dock in the Pearl Harbor navy yard when the attack began. She was one of the first ships to open fire as enemy dive and torpedo bombers roared out of the high overcast. Japanese aircraft did not succeed in repeated attempts to torpedo the dry dock, but *Pennsylvania* and the surrounding dock areas were severely strafed. The crew of one 5 inch gun mount was wiped out when a bomb struck the starboard side of her boat deck and exploded.

Destroyers Cassin and Downes, just forward of *Pennsylvania* in the dry dock, were seriously damaged by bomb hits. *Pennsylvania* was pockmarked by flying fragments. A part of a torpedo tube from *Downes*, about 1,000 lb in weight, was blown onto the forecastle of *Pennsylvania*. She had 15 men killed (including her executive officer), 14 missing in action, and 38 wounded.

Mr. Irwin was assigned to the USS Pennsylvania. When the attack began, his first thought was that it was an exercise, but that notion was quickly dispelled. He was at an island barracks since the ship was in dry dock, and hopped onto a truck for a quick ride to the harbor. Bob Irwin responded to a call for volunteers to bring up ammunition from below decks for a 5 inch gun used as an anti-aircraft weapon.

Before Mr. Irwin went below, he saw three bombs fall from a Japanese plane onto the USS Arizona, and watched as one of those bombs penetrated the Arizona's deck, striking the magazine. He witnessed the complete destruction of the Arizona that resulted in more than 1,100 of her crewmembers being killed. The catastrophic explosion is his lasting, most vivid memory. Among the killed, missing and wounded on his own ship, the Pennsylvania, were many of his friends.

The *USS Patterson* was a destroyer moored at Pearl Harbor when the Japanese carrier-based planes swooped in. Her gunners sped to battle stations, opened fire, and blasted one enemy plane out of the sky. Within an hour the destroyermen were searching for possible enemy submarines off the harbor entrance.

Following the attack, *Patterson* patrolled the Hawaiian Sea Frontier in the screen of aircraft carrier Saratoga without finding trace of the enemy. On 28 December, returning from patrol, she rescued 19 survivors of merchant ship *Marimi* adrift for several days after having been torpedoed by a Japanese submarine.

Mr. Schatz was a Patterson crewmember. He'd never been allowed to

actually fire the .50 caliber machine gun he volunteered to man during the attack. Previously, the only persons who'd operated it were experienced hands so that better scores were achieved by the ship during graded drills. Those older hands, though, were caught up in the repair of a boiler. The sight of buildings exploding on nearby Ford Island immediately convinced him the event was the real thing. Quickly, he found the machine gun was easy to aim since every fifth round was a "tracer" which had a definite color he could see.

What he remembers best? Ewalt Schatz said a Japanese plane passed overhead so close that he looked right into the pilot's face and saw him so well, he thought he might recognize him if he ever met him on the street, or from pictures, in later years. Try as he might, though, he never has. Mr. Schatz believed then the pilot was looking directly at him, although across time he concluded the pilot was more likely intensely studying the ship as a target.

Mr. Schatz was credited as the USS Patterson gunner who shot a Japanese plane out of the sky. It was a different plane from the one in which he looked so closely into the pilot's face.

The two gentlemen were gracious, humble, and retain a great sense of humor. Mr. Irwin still flies his own small plane, an Aeronca. Mr. Schatz, in reference to his having shot down a plane, remarked: "Heck, it may be true or not. A lot of our people were shooting at those planes besides me." I gave up my seat between them to an Australian lady, and they were happy to welcome her in my place. True Navy men, both still like the pretty girls!

It was a privilege on December 7, 2012, to represent you, the good people of Cloudcroft, New Mexico, in thanking these men for their courageous actions on December 7, 1941. They struck me as regular good citizens, patriotic, who acted with bravery under fire, caught up in an extraordinary event they still remember well.

May God bless them, and all of you, in this New Year of 2013!

39

Of Jerry Heinzelmann, Village Hardware and Nancy Nice the Cat

April 2013

There are certain good and enduring moments one experiences which are associated intimately with Cloudcroft, thoughts that won't ever go away. What are yours? Here's just a few of mine.

In 1993 during my first visit, driving in from the east and experiencing the unexpected beauty of the region, transitioning from high desert to mountainous terrain.

During that same drive, being passed by a sheriff's deputy, who was driving of all things a pickup truck. I was a city police officer who drove cars. I want to drive a truck and work in this beautiful place, I thought, and within four years was being sworn in by Sheriff Johnny Lee, to be a deputy sheriff for more than seven years in the Sacramentos.

More than six inches of unexpected snow fell during that first trip. Just seeing the pure beauty of it, and feeling the crispness and freshness of the air.

Seeing a deer and her fawn quietly cross the road near Silver, Saddle and Apache Campgrounds on Highway 244, during another snowstorm.

Later, hiking a trail in that same area, in a heavy but gentle snow, experiencing a quiet so peaceful and noteworthy I could actually hear the flakes hitting the ground.

Cresting Prestridge Hill into the awe of Hay Canyon.

Likewise, topping Hornbuckle Hill, above Timberon, with a view so majestic I could see west to Las Cruces, to the south to El Paso.

Watching Friday night football games in the tiny high school arena that formerly existed along Highway 82 within the village, the field lights on. Where it seemed the games should be played.

Having my daughter, who was in Nebraska, come to me during a visit when she was 15 and say: "Dad, I want to live here with you and Cynthia, go to school here." Seeing that happen.

Watching her and her teammates win a volleyball tournament in Capitan, against all odds, a sensational comeback. Cloudcroft, the perennial underdog, the champs!

Watching my daughter ascend the stand at the University of New Mexico in 2002, receiving the award as state champion in discus; then soon, seeing her graduate from CHS, 5th in her class, an educational turnaround for her, thanks to her teachers here.

Annually, the gathering of a Christmas tree in the forest.

There are so many more good moments. These are but a few that have bonded my soul to the fabric of this community as if it has been fastened with Liquid Nails.

A typical Cloudcroft stay for a person not born here - who comes after "retirement" - is at most 15 to 20 years. The smart ones realize it's not important what you did before, but what you do to contribute positively once you arrive.

Some other folks who rolled in about the same time were Jerry and Carolyn Heinzelmann. They've always said they found "their little bit of heaven". Jerry, a graduate of the University of Oklahoma and without doubt, a Sooner fan, had been a petroleum geologist all his working life. But he wasn't a geologist in Cloudcroft.

Jerry became a merchant, the local hardware store owner. He became involved in village politics, heading up Planning & Zoning. He very nearly became the mayor, once losing by just a few votes. He worked for the good of this village.

His first store was on Mexican Avenue. He moved it to the rear of the Cookshack building. Then he opened it in its present location. Each store was a place you could sit down and talk with Jerry, be welcomed as a friend. One could pet Nancy the Cat. You were always welcomed by a true gentleman who loved Cloudcroft.

Jerry, of course, had his own intimate thoughts of our mountaintop. I don't know what all of them were.

But he became a good friend. His leadership and patience guided me when I sat as a member of Planning & Zoning. He was there for me during times of trouble. He and Carolyn hosted my family and friends, gave comfort to my wife and children. Before and after, he gave me employment at Village Hardware, the trust of having his keys and access to his bank account much more important than the pay. Then, I fed Nancy the Cat.

Jerry visited me in prison, the first person to do so, braving a scary environment that many people wouldn't face. What a thrill it was to greet him!

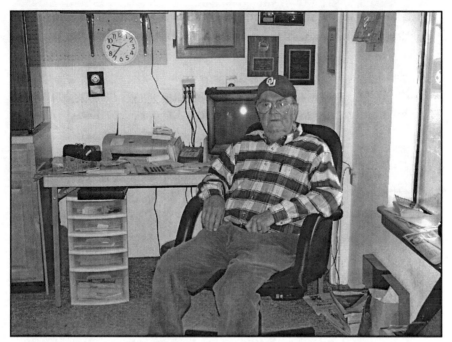

Village Hardware's Jerry Heinzelmann in his original store on Mexican Avenue. The OU ball cap rules!

Afterwards, he had his own troubles, losing a foot. I drove him to El Paso for doctor's visits and watched as he courageously struggled with rehab. We ate lunch there at his favorite restaurants, laughed and joked as he smiled in spite of his physical hardships. I got to know him pretty well, and appreciated him more and more.

Ole Father Time is a tough taskmaster to everyone. Jerry's increased need for medical attention and his and Carolyn's desire to be closer to family ended their Cloudcroft cycle, as those things do for many. About four years ago, they left their little bit of heaven behind for others beginning their own Cloudcroft love affair.

They moved to Ft. Worth. We stayed in touch. During 2011 I visited with Jerry and Carolyn at one of their favorite restaurants in Dallas, on Mockingbird Lane. Jerry had been to a doctor's visit, but we laughed

and talked again. They did the best they could with their move, but Cloudcroft was foremost in their thoughts. It would be the last time I'd see him.

Gerald "Jerry" Heinzelmann Jr. died last month on Friday, March 1st, with his family gathered around. Cloudcroft lost a good one.

Thank you, Jerry for what you meant to me and mine. God bless you, Carolyn and family, as you go forward. What a gentleman Gerald Heinzelmann was! He's an integral part of the intimate thoughts of mine mentioned above which bind me forever to this community, and these words are dedicated to his memory.

40

Slipping and Sliding
on the Casino Freeway

May 2013

Drive the same stretch of asphalt over several years in the Sacramento Mountains where roads are curvy and anything but level...mix in weather and animals and fellow drivers...and you're sure to have some tales to tell.

Such are my experiences with the 30 miles of State Road 244 from U. S. Highway 82 over to U. S. Highway 70. The Casino Freeway.

Certainly you have your own recollections of this drive. Late at night, the area can resemble Jurassic Park. I recall one person having to repair a turkey dent.

A few days ago, returning to Cloudcroft from Ruidoso, I scribbled some notes as I passed certain memory points, meanwhile trying not to create another. If numbering backwards bothers you, just read this upside down.

Mile Marker 28. A herd of wild horses dashed out in front of me. Or at least a herd of domesticated horses, having a wild party. Why don't horses ever act like that during the daytime?

Mile Marker 23. Dead Man's Curve, where the guard rails are. Most memories of that spot were generated from drivers headed northbound, especially motorcycle riders. When law enforcement officers were given an accident to respond to at an unknown place on 244, the default location was Dead Man's Curve, very appropriately named.

The story was that the Mescalero Apache notched a pine tree near that curve for each fatality. I never saw that tree, but maybe it got notched so much it fell.

Mile Marker 22 through 17. Four years ago, an ungrateful human dumped a dog in that area. The devoted dog stayed three months. Refusing all efforts to be rescued, it waited patiently for its master, who didn't deserve him. More than one of us left food. The pup would approach strangers within a few feet, but then retreat. I tried to catch it several times, but couldn't. I don't know of its fate. Hopefully there was a good outcome.

Mile Marker 21. Driving to Ruidoso in 1997, I found the coldest patch of air I personally ever encountered in the mountains. It was 15 degrees below zero.

Mile Marker 16. As I motored northbound, a bull elk bailed off a hill to my right, landing directly in front of my car. Realizing its situation, it lost footing as it hunkered down trying to get traction. There was a lot of hunkering going on. I hunkered down on the brakes. We both stopped, the elk centered in front of my Jeep Cherokee, appearing every bit the hood ornament, just his head and antlers visible. But there were no hits, no runs, no further errors. The panic gone, he got up slowly and trotted away, pausing once to turn and stare are me indignantly. Embarrassed, probably. Or maybe mad.

Mile Marker 18 through 13. Remember the sunflowers, around the year 2000? The entire valley of Elk Canyon was covered with waist-high giant sunflowers. Beautiful, just a yellow sea of color! Never before, never since, in the 17 years I've been around.

Mile Marker 17. One night an owl, standing on the roadway, took flight at my approach. The weather was warm. My window was down, my left arm on the windowsill. The owl nearly flew inside my car, its wingtip brushing my shoulder. It didn't seem so wise at the moment.

Mile Marker 10. More wild horses suddenly thundering across the road, in the dark of course. Probably just horsing around.

Mile Marker 7. One loose horse, domesticated version. A big beautiful white thing. I was dispatched to round it up. Ha! As I stood perplexed, the owner appeared, rattled a feed can with a few oats, and the wayward horse trotted over. So that's how it's done. Live and learn.

Mile Marker 7. Didn't witness it, but a small airplane landed during a snowstorm, on a curved runway. (The white horse was gone). The plane remained parked a week, then the owner came and flew it away. No one had bothered it. No kidding.

Mile Marker 5. Returning from Ruidoso after midnight, having completed my shift as an officer in the Downs, encountered an undersized Texas car in an oversized New Mexico snowstorm. The young couple had a sleeping eight year old daughter, were low on gasoline, in the wrong place in the wrong kind of vehicle. They'd driven in from Artesia, bound for Ruidoso, hadn't realized Cloudcroft was just around the corner from Hwy 82 and Road 244. I've never seen people happier to see a cop. They followed me to Allsup's for fuel, then wisely spent the night in our village.

Mile Marker 2. A large travel trailer over the edge. Joe Mancillas' little wrecker wouldn't budge it. Big Mamma was called from Ruidoso,

but the driver wasn't' experienced in mountain towing. Forced to watch, Joe was having a cat. "Would you let Joe try?" I asked. Yes. Joe played Big Mamma like a fine violin and had the trailer up muy pronto.

The little red Cloudcroft wrecker works hard to clear Hwy 244 at Mile Marker 2.

Mile Marker 1 and one-half. In a snowstorm, watched a doe move quietly across the road with her fawn, leaving silent hoof prints. A peaceful, unforgettable scene.

Mile Marker 1 and one-half, later. Guns stolen from our museum were recovered from behind a log just 20 feet off the edge of 244, after the suspects confessed. The guns had been stashed behind and under the big log. We'd ridden by often over many months wondering where those weapons were. The log is still there, the weapons are not. They were cleaned and returned to the museum.

Mile Marker 1. A car went over the side, narrowly missed a small pine, and the tree had to be cut to haul the car back up, no other choice.

Kept that little pine for a Charlie Brown kind of Christmas tree, and it was a good one. That was nine years ago.

There are others, but we're already back at Highway 82.

God provided a beautiful setting for those 30 miles, and He's always kindly given me safe passage under some pretty tough conditions. I'm thankful.

41

Cloudcroft to the Atlantic Ocean!
Swan Song of the Shasta...

June 2013

By chance, do you know what U.S. roadway is designated the Jefferson Davis Memorial Highway? Which is the South Georgia Parkway? Through Sherman, Texas, the Buck Owens Freeway?

To us, U.S Highway 82 is a small two-lane road without shoulders, the road we take to Allsup's. We may have gone to Lubbock via 82, but from there it disappears into a cloud of West Texas dust. Well, surprise, surprise. Our little Route 82 actually proceeds uninterrupted for 1,700 miles to the east coast of the USA. It starts at Brunswick, Georgia, at its intersection with Interstate 95...just six miles from the Atlantic Ocean! It's the answer to all those questions above.

From an elevation of just 11 feet in Brunswick, westbound it ascends to Cloudcroft's 8,650 feet before it plummets some 4,000 feet to Alamogordo, a plummet we're very familiar with!

Portions of New Mexico, Texas, Arkansas, Mississippi, Alabama

and Georgia are transversed. While some larger cities are along its path - Lubbock, Wichita Falls, Sherman and Texarkana in Texas; Montgomery in Alabama - basically it's a trip through Small Town America. Hundreds of little towns and villages dominate.

Mile Zero is at Alamogordo's intersection of Highways 82/54/70. I've had a bucket list item saying "make this trip from one end to the other" for a couple of years until now. I check marked that item on April 28th, 2013, having started in Alamo on April 16 th. My desire was to discover interesting people, places and things along the route, primarily in all those small towns. And yes, I found them.

My 1956 Shasta "canned ham" travel trailer, always a conversation starter, followed along. Sadly, after eight years, this was the last trip for The Egg, now replaced by a 20 footer with a bathroom. The Shasta and I have seen a lot of places in the rear view mirror.

Why make this trip? Well, for fun of course, but this community has given me much, and maybe I could partly return the favor by writing a travelogue promoting RV travel, I thought, since tourism is our bread and butter. Lisa King at the Chamber of Commerce cooperated, and I passed out a few hundred Cloudcroft brochures along the way.

On the starting date, my friend Alan Lochner of Cloudcroft took photos of The Egg and me in Alamo. Doing the trip from west to east is an advantage, isn't it? With a downhill drop of nearly two miles in altitude, surely it's a way to save gas.

In 1975, Al drove Highway 82 on a motorcycle. He remembers a visit with a gas station owner in New Boston, Texas, near Arkansas. I left with a description of the station. Since it's been 38 years, more than likely the building was long since gone.

Pausing briefly in Cloudcroft at the Chamber, I pressed on. Another short delay at Mile Marker 51 near Elk found me saying a little prayer

for safe travel. I often pull over there to reflect on the worst traffic crash I ever worked as a law enforcement officer, feeling the presence of the six 15 year old girls who were killed in a church bus accident those 13 years ago. My "travel angels" were invited along. Since my trip was accident free, maybe they came.

Another necessary stop out that way is Tom and Pam Runyan's fruit stand. I wanted to take some Tularosa cherry cider along, and say so long to the camel and buffalo.

Thus began a two week routine of daily travel - interviews - good eating - photos - sightseeing - museums - u-turning - discovery - eventual arrival at a RV park, then nightly Internet research for the next day's journey.

Folks, it's this simple…every place has a story, and someone who'll tell it. You just have to find the storyteller, and ask. Many were heard. There's space here for only a few.

I found 56 MPH winds in West Texas, an RV park owner -the city judge - who recommended I leave my little trailer hooked to my heavier truck that might serve as an anchor. Good advice. I heard tall tales at museums and listened to Mississippi blues music; visited Elvis's birthplace in Tupelo, Mississippi; ate the World's Best BBQ at the A-1 Pawn Shop in Smackover, Arkansas: and saw civil rights hotspots of the 1960s in Greenville, Mississippi, and Montgomery, Alabama.

Passing through New Boston, Texas…an old service station building meeting Al Lochner's description caught my eye. I turned around, found an Arkansas man removing memorabilia to take home. He was the grandson of the long-deceased owner. Emailing Al a photo, I got this excited response: "That's it!"

Animals weren't to be outdone. Kermit the Frog's home was along the way, as were miniature horses in Georgia. Vanessa in Centreville,

Alabama, told me of seeing her dog Christmas sucked out of a hole in the roof during a tornado two years ago, as she and four others desperately held on…and of how in a true Christmas miracle, her pup came picking his way back through the rubble a few minutes later.

My tour guide in Montgomery was my old friend and FBI National Academy classmate, Alabama's U.S. Marshall Art Baylor, formerly Montgomery's police chief. Touring his office was the first time I'd ever been in a federal building that big when I wasn't in big trouble.

Remember the TV show, Bonanza? Two of its stars were born along the route. DeKalb, Texas, was the home of Dan Blocker who played Hoss Cartwright. (Later, I'd pass through Acton, Georgia, the birthplace of Pernell Roberts who portrayed Hoss's brother Adam.) In DeKalb, my tour guide, again a city judge - good thing I didn't have any active warrants - took me to Dan Blocker's grave site. Hoss was loved in DeKalb, down to earth, very unpretentious. His ordinary tombstone is much visited.

In 1985, singer Ricky Nelson, son of Ozzie and Harriet, was killed in a plane crash just a mile south of DeKalb. Her Honor drove me to the site, then showed me the tail section of the airplane - an old C-47 - stored in the local museum.

Don't be fooled by its two lanes and no shoulders in New Mexico. U.S. Highway 82 is an awesome road along much of its length. Close to 70% is four-laned, with more being completed. Only in portions of Alabama and Georgia did I find roadway similar to ours. Though RV parks were sometimes in short supply, it's a great road system to travel for the purposes I had.

Seeing something that interested me, I only had to go a short distance to turn around since access wasn't limited as on an Interstate.

Dekalb TX City Judge Joanie Haldeman with Dan Blocker's life-size cutout at the Williams House Museum.

I arrived in Brunswick, Georgia, on Sunday, April 28[th], at noon, and parked The Egg next to a very large sister on Georgia's Jekyll Island, within a few hundred feet of the Atlantic Ocean. A great trip! On Friday, May 17[th], new owners Crickett and Tony of Vero Beach, Florida, took possession of the 1956 Shasta, following an eBay auction. Thanks, girl, you were a faithful friend.

Sure, you can get your kicks on Route 66, but there's much more to do on Route 82. Please stay tuned for the book. Profits will be designated to a worthy Cloudcroft charity.

The '56 Shasta, The Egg, next to a big brother, gazes at the Atlantic Ocean, journey completed.

42

Brother, Can You Spare
a Dollar (Store)?

July 2013

"Oh, no, not in Cloudcroft!" she exclaimed. Talking to her in a faraway North Texas town, I was surprised she knew of our village.

The director of her Chamber of Commerce, she explained her family has an annual reunion here. Telling her of the Family Dollar issue, she reacted as above, and it surprised me. After all, isn't her job...well... the promotion of commerce? And her town has both a Family Dollar and a Dollar General.

"Why not?" I asked. She answered like this: "Well, Cloudcroft is a special place. It just won't look right there."

Won't look right? Isn't that a big part of the controversy? Everyone has an opinion and I'm no exception. Please allow me to put my mouth where my money has been.

During 2011 an opportunity presented itself for me to satisfy a long

time goal, ownership of a weekly newspaper. One became available and I'm traveling extensively, so I visited and worked salary free for a few weeks to learn the ropes. The little Cloudcroft-sized town already had a Dollar General.

I had no plans to permanently relocate but I spent about a third of my time there in my small travel trailer. A remote log-in computer service gave me everywhere access to business records, including payroll, through Quickbooks. So I took the plunge.

The usual problems of managing a little enterprise were multiplied by distance. After only 15 months of ownership, a buyer appeared so I sold the newspaper six months ago.

Good for you, you might say, but what's the point? Good question.

The town was economically depressed, having lost its major employer, a big industrial plant, about five years ago. Time were and are tough. But it still had a full service grocery store, a Mercantile if you will, which had been in place for 70 years. Full service to me means including meat and produce departments.

During my tenure as publisher, a Family Dollar opened. Except for the owner of the old grocery store, it wasn't a disturbing event. Appearance isn't paramount there. The FD had the standard red garish look, only matched, it seems, by the yellow gaudiness of the DG stores.

But the grocery store soon folded. Chuck, the owner, simply couldn't compete with the corporate buying power of both "mini-Walmarts". Chuck had been an advertiser in our paper.

Companies like Family Dollar and Dollar General are very large, powerful corporations. Have you seen one of their regional distribution centers? Every business in Cloudcroft would fit inside one, at the same time.

The dollar stores took lots of money away but with the big exception of gross receipts tax and the few jobs, they didn't give much back in the way of community involvement. They also have no real meat and produce departments. No one understands that better than people who live in Cloudcroft.

Do you like Walmart? Whether you do or don't, they're community minded. Girl Scouts can sell cookies, the Salvation Army - a great organization, by the way - can ring their bells on the parking lot. You didn't see that happening at the dollar stores. Our closest Walmart, incidentally, was 28 miles away.

The new Family Dollar provided a salaried store manager's job which paid a decent amount plus benefits, and the manager, Virginia, became a friend. She's good at her job but works mega-hours, practically living at the store. There's an assistant manager's job with lower pay but with benefits, and four or five other workers toiling for lower wages. FD's part-time workers are eligible for cafeteria-style benefits.

Corporate stores are run by strict rules, and the ability to place ads in local newspapers isn't an option the local manager has. The affairs of dollar stores are directed from afar by some mysterious regional person. We received no advertising - a newspaper's bread and butter - from either dollar store. Our only opportunity for monetary gain was to stuff Dollar General's sales flyers into our papers, a time-intensive effort that paid so little it wasn't worth the labor cost.

The opening of the Family Dollar was a news event, though, and we covered it. Later, we even featured Virginia and her store in a Business of the Month-type story.

I've always shopped at the dollar stores. The pricing, convenience of parking, and less crowded conditions are features I like. Family Dollar has been my favorite for some unknown reason, and the store on Florida Avenue in Alamogordo has seen its fair share of my money.

And yes, as the newspaper owner, I bought the usual things a business needed like paper products and cleaning supplies at the dollar stores, mostly at FD. It sure beat a 56 mile round trip to the Walmart.

My problem with having one here? Like the lady in the North Texas town, I think Cloudcroft is a special place and a Family Dollar with the standard appearance just won't look right.

Village staff tells me that preliminary talks with Family Dollar have pointed out motif requirements, things that have to be abided by. That worries me a bit, having lived here and knowing what Allsup's looks like..how the Post Office was built…First National Bank's new building…the new school. Motif is defined as "the main theme" and is more than signage.

But gasoline is expensive. Driving mountain roads can be dangerous. Convenience is great, as is availability and pricing of products. Gross receipts tax collection is important. And it's a jungle out there, folks, with the law of the jungle being - adapt or die. I've said this before… the only constant in life is change.

If…the Cloudcroft "special place" look can be maintained, I support having a Family Dollar here. I don't care what the inside of the store looks like. It's the outside that potentially bothers me.

If it happens, you can say goodbye to the Mercantile forever. They simply couldn't sell enough pies to stay alive. And I hope I'm wrong, but I doubt the Mountain Monthly will benefit with new advertising.

Other cities have faced similar problems. Gettysburg, Pennsylvania, is one. For all I know, there's a dollar store looking seriously at the ground of Pickett's Charge.

Columbia, Maryland, a place I've visited several times, is a good case study. Developed in the 1960s, commercial centers are essentially hidden from view by berms, trees and shrubbery.

Per Wikipedia, Columbia's nine 'village centers' provide residents with nearby shopping as well, often including supermarkets, gas stations, liquor stores, dry cleaners, restaurants, and hair salons. The village centers are laid out so that individual stores are not visible from the road, unlike traditional strip malls. The arrangement is criticized because it makes it difficult for newcomers and non-residents to know what shopping is available; it is praised for eliminating much of the garishness of roadside America.

Maybe they have what we're looking for. A cake store that doesn't look like a cake store where you can buy your cake at a good price, and eat it too. And without driving too far, the icing on the cake.

Just food for thought.

43

Horsing Around With the Pain-In-The-Neck Board

September 2013

Ask people to name the person most associated with horses in Cloudcroft and most likely they'll say Carl Wood. Carl, a good friend, ran pony rides here in recent years, and his horses pulled tourists around the village in a wagon.

But ask either visitors or locals with some silver in their hair who was the King of the Cloudcroft Cowboys 40 years or more ago and they'll remember George Tally. If you came to Cloudcroft between 1927 and 1974 and rode a horse around town, the critter came from Mr. Tally's barn and corral.

George Tally passed away in 1974. He was 69 years old. His corral is gone. But his barn is still standing, at 97 Mescalero Trail. It's the second structure behind the King's Treasure thrift store on Burro Street. There's a concrete wall around its base.

Mr. Tally kept about 50 horses in his barn and in his corral, which

was located about 200 feet downhill to the west from the barn. It was behind the present location of Green Mountain Real Estate, in the triangular confluence of Osha Trail and Mexican Avenue. He also had horses at the many children's camps throughout the mountain area.

George Tally was born with club feet and couldn't walk normally. At the age of two, an operation was attempted to correct his problems but it wasn't successful. For the rest of his life, he had difficulty walking and wore special shoes. So he was one of the rare cowboys who didn't wear cowboy boots, since he couldn't.

He had difficulty walking on his feet, that is. Mr. Tally compensated for his lack of "foot walking" by learning to walk on his hands and arms, which he built into powerful appendages. On his hands, he could out walk most people who were using their feet!

In the early days, one could ride a horse throughout Cloudcroft. Yes, if you had a burro, you could actually ride it down Burro Street. But more cars and faster traffic eventually created an unsafe situation, and the horses' propensity to leave gifts of fruit laying about – horse apples – finally caused the village to enact an ordinance banning them.

Mr. Tally's horses then could only be taken for a ride on the Osha Trail.

I said George Tally's corral is gone. It is. As late as 2007, though, remnants of it still stood. It and an adjacent shack had collapsed and were an eyesore. I had a handyman business at the time and was contracted to tear all of it down and haul away the residue. I did.

But, a weathered board about 10 feet long had been nailed up as a sort of headboard over the corral, and it had an unusual shape that caught my eye. The ends were sawn at 45 degree angles and had old nail holes in them. I just couldn't bring myself to toss it.

It was the kind of old barn wood one might have made a fireplace

mantel out of if it had been thicker. Someday, I thought, I'd find a good use for it. So I stashed it in my shop, where it's sat these last six years.

In the latter stage of George Tally's life, his daughter, Nettie, came to work for him, though she'd always helped out. She worked fulltime for her father from 1972 – 1974. Nettie, as you might guess, was an expert with horses, winning numerous competitions in barrel racing, for example.

In 1962 she was Miss New Mexico State Fair. Through the 1980s, she was a force in rodeo in the Southwest, winning many awards including embossed saddles. As a child, she lived on Alamo Peak at the Forest Service fire tower. Her dad and mother, Jeannette, operated it. Her mother worked the tower while George fought fires, and carried on his horse – of course – business.

Enter 2013. Having been a long-time fan of the Barn Door Café, I was happy to see it reopen after it'd been shuttered for a couple of years. I've met Mr. Horton who was the original owner, and the reason the area is still known by some old-timers as Hortonville. He still summers in the area, still visits the café.

James and Shirley Summers, parents of Cloudcroft police officer Kevin Summers, ran the café for some time. There have been other owners. The new operators are Vernon and Nettie Fleming. And yes, Nettie Fleming is the former Nettie Tally!

Included amongst rodeo memorabilia on the walls and staircase is an oil painting of Nettie's dad, George Tally. In 1970, he was the chosen subject of the annual Cloudcroft Art Class, conducted during the summer at the high school, and it's an excellent portrait of him.

Nettie said her dad had been both a good guy and a bad guy. He wrangled horses for the 1967-68 western television show, Cimarron Strip,

starring actor Stuart Whitman, filmed in Las Cruces. George Tally rode as an extra. In one episode, she explained, the good guys were waiting on horses to cross the Rio Grande, and George Tally was wearing a white hat. In the next scene, the bad guys were on the other side of the Rio Grande waiting to get the good guys, and once again there was her father, this time wearing a black hat!

Among other talents, Nettie's husband Vernon Fleming is an expert rodeo photographer and many framed photos on the wall attest to his skills. They've owned "seven or eight" cafes in the past.

As we talked, the old board came to mind and I wondered to myself if Nettie might like to have it. After all, it was most likely her father who nailed it to the corral, and both of them would have walked under it many times.

"I have something you might like," I told her, and retrieved it from my shop.

"Oh my goodness!" she exclaimed on seeing it, for the first time in almost 40 years. "That's my pain-in-the-neck board. I sure do remember it." "Why do you call it that?" I asked.

She said the horses, when being lined up in the corral for a trail ride, would sometimes toss their heads around, bridles going a'flying, and hanging up on the pointed end of the board. "It was a pain in the neck to get the bridles off that board," she said. Nevertheless, she seemed very pleased to have it back.

The board will be refinished and displayed on the restaurant wall. Sometimes the Good Lord gives us a chance to do a little something good for someone, even accidentally, and I'm grateful now that I kept it.

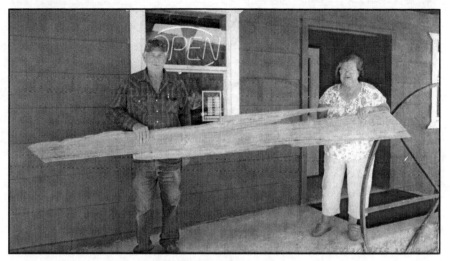

Vernon and Nettie Fleming hold the Pain-In-The-Neck board at the Barn Door Café, 2013.

After all this time, the pain-in-the-neck board has once again gotten itself corralled!

44

A Working Visit to Chama and the Cumbres & Toltec Scenic Railroad

October 2013

"Got a moon and a million stars
The sound of steel and old box cars
The thought of you driving me insane
Come on baby let's go listen to the night train."

So sings country star Jason Aldean in his current hit, "Night Train". Not many things are more alluring or in tune with romance than the sound of a faraway train. And he doesn't even mention the magic of a train whistle, music to the soul!

New Mexico is home to one of the most soulful steam train whistles around, that of the Cumbres & Toltec Scenic Railroad. If you haven't been to Chama to see it…ride it…experience both its charm and grandeur…you're missing one of the true enchantments in this Land of Same!

In past years, I'd ridden the Cumbres & Toltec two times. Having done

so, I wanted to do something more to help preserve this beautiful piece of history. So a bucket list item was created. My wife and I joined the railroad's Friends Support Committee two years ago and this past July and August, spent time in Chama getting 'er done.

Chama began in 1865, the year the Civil War ended. It was just a small settlement by the Rio Chama River. It had a couple of stores, some saloons (a necessity in the West), a blacksmith shop, and a tent hotel. In 1870 it got its first sawmill. In December 1880, the railroad arrived, and is still there.

The steam locomotives in use today were built in Philadelphia, Pennsylvania, during the 1920s. Yes, and they're still chugging up Cumbres Pass, a mountain over 10,000 feet tall! Engine #487 has never worked anywhere else. The Cumbres & Toltec is America's longest, highest and most scenic steam train, and also its most authentic.

The CTSR still operates over 64 miles from Chama, New Mexico, to Antonito, Colorado. The line, built in 1880, is an engineering feat. National Historical Designation was received earlier this year.

There were seven one-week volunteer work sessions this past summer. People from across the United States came to help, at no pay. Some repaired old railcars, others painted those already restored. States represented were New Mexico and Colorado, of course, but also California, Missouri, Alabama, Florida, Arizona, Mississippi and New York. About 50 persons, including a Canadian, were present for each of the two sessions we attended.

My wife worked in food preparation, and as an exhibit hall guide. I acted as a chronicler, documenting the progress of projects through written accounts and photographs.

In years past, the Cumbres & Toltec was part of the Denver & Rio Grande Railroad which ran between Alamosa and Denver, Colorado,

and down to Santa Fe. It supported various mining operations, logging, and oil drilling activities.

Since 1970, it's been a historical narrow gauge railroad for passenger traffic, and actually we share the CTSR with Colorado. A commission of persons from both states administers its affairs.

 Chama is a beautiful place in the mountains, much so because of its similarity to Cloudcroft. The village's altitude is 7,800 feet. Like Cloudcroft, temperatures were only in the 80s during daytime, and down to the 40s after sundown. Most nights, a heater or a blanket felt good.

What we did won't change the world, but it was fun to have a small part in helping continue this little slice of history. The real heroes? The hard workers who toiled years ago to build a railroad in places you can't believe until you look over the edge of a cliff 800 feet down into Toltec Gorge, way up in the Rocky Mountains. The northern New Mexico and southern Colorado landscape is nothing short of awesome!

As often happens, we found ammunition for the Small World Cannon in Chama. Noting my home state as Mississippi, our greeter said: "Oh, Billy and Arlene Crider are from Mississippi. There they are now." So I moseyed over.

Billy Crider is 75, 6'4" tall, and has the true Southern gift of gab. His wife, Arlene, and I grew up in the same Mississippi county. Our fathers were born within a three week period in 1916, their homes 10 miles apart, and knew each other. Arlene's mother is 92 and remembers my dad, who would be 97 now. She's been to New Mexico and ridden the Cumbres & Toltec.

There was more. Billy's father and my grandfather both worked for the Illinois Central Railroad out of McComb, Mississippi, a stop still made by the ICR's legendary "City of New Orleans", the passenger train made famous by singers like Arlo Guthrie and Willie Nelson.

The Criders have gone to Chama for the last 15 years as summer volunteers. She's worked as a chronicler. Billy works as a docent, a person who rides the train, is familiar with its history and that of the towns along its route. He answers visitors' questions with ease!

The Friends' web site at www.cumbrestoltec.org features two live webcams at the Chama rail yard. One faces north, the other south. The small yellow building at the left of the image on the north camera, much like our Cloudcroft Chamber of Commerce, was a bunkhouse built in 1881. It's now used as a computer center and was my work location.

And yes, there's still time during 2013 to ride! The current season runs through Sunday, October 20th. Information on schedules can be found at www.cumbrestoltec.com or by calling 1-800-286-2737. The lunch at the midpoint of the trip at Osier, Colorado, along the Rio de Los Pinos River, is to die for, incidentally. Rides during 2014 begin in April.

CNN has voted riding on the Cumbres & Toltec Scenic Railroad as one of its "49 Journeys That Will Change Your Life". Why not change yours? And say hello to Billy and Arlene for us.

Locomotive 489, built in 1925, arrives with style from Osier, Colorado, happy folks aboard!

When the train with happy folks aboard including many children, came chugging in daily at 4 pm, pulled by a big steam locomotive, it was a beautiful sight. "...the sound of steel and old box cars..." And what an awe-inspiring whistle! We thank the Good Lord for the strength and opportunity to have done this.

45

Listening to the Hoofbeats of Extraordinary Lives

November 2013

We who had children in Cloudcroft schools know of K-Bob's Steakhouse in Socorro, New Mexico, especially if our kids were athletes. The restaurant has a special dining room for team busses going to places like Albuquerque, to such events as state track meets.

Victories were celebrated in K-Bob's back room, defeats were mulled over. The food was always good, though, whatever the game outcome. Most of the kids and adults ate hamburgers or chicken fried steaks. Oddly, though, my favorite there has always been - fried shrimp.

Shrimp? Such seafood certainly isn't native to New Mexico, since we have much beach but no ocean. "Where are we?" those shrimp must wonder, arriving from Maine or the Gulf of Mexico. Like people, they probably have to be reminded that our state is really one of the United States, the one that fills in the blank spot between Texas and Arizona.

Since the shrimp don't grow up within walking distance, they're likely

delivered frozen. But anything will thaw out here, and shrimp do so nicely. When prepared, they're delicious.

Besides knowing that shrimp taste great at K-Bob's, I know there's a good story most anyplace, and K-Bob's wouldn't be an exception. During a recent visit, I admired a mural on the wall. It depicts the old Santa Fe Trail. I commented about it to the lady who ushered shrimp to my table.

While they filled out their last wills and testaments, she and I chatted. "Wouldn't it be something to have traveled that route back then?" I mused. Her response? "My husband and I did that sort of thing for years, between here and Arizona, on horses. Later, we made the journey in a wagon."

Wasn't that a long way to ride a horse? "About 500 miles," she answered. Seemed to me to be an invitation to visit a doctor who specializes in saddle sores. "Can you give me a quick rundown on your experiences?" I asked.

It was mid-afternoon, things were slow, and soon she had a few moments to spare. Since then, we've exchanged more information. Her name is Elena Marshall. Her husband died a couple of years ago. She wants to write a book about their adventures. She kept diaries, good written records.

Elena and John, her husband, grew up in Massachusetts. When she was nine, her sister acquired a horse, and Elena developed an itch to ride which persisted. After marrying, she introduced John to horses. They weren't satisfied with life in the Northeast and boldly headed west in 1984, all their earthly possessions packed in his old car. "A jalopy," she says.

They thought their names too "Eastern", so they adopted new ones, Buster (Elena) and Cody (John). Arriving, they found work on a dude

ranch near Flagstaff, then worked a circuit of such ranches over New Mexico and Arizona. They decided to work summers here and winter over in Arizona. They had little money and few possessions but had three good horses.

Those horses were Buster (not to be confused with the human Buster, who was really Elena), Pookie, and Rushmore. The first trip was made in 1986 from actor Gabby Hayes' ranch west of Lemitar, New Mexico, over to Phoenix. Lemitar is just north of Socorro. That journey extended over a period of 101 days that summer into fall. Twenty-five days were spent actually traveling.

The rest of the time? Buster (the human) and Cody, really John, worked along the way to buy food, both for the animals and themselves, of course. The days spent not traveling were full, unloading hay, mending fence, checking windmills, shoeing horses.

In 1987, Elena's father, George Terrell, wrote about that trip for the Foxboro, Massachusetts, newspaper, The Reporter. "The grub line in action," he called their ride.

From Lemitar, it took them to Magdalena to Pie Town to Quemado… along the outskirts of the Gila National Forest…into Arizona to Alpine and Greer and the Fort Apache Indian Reservation…over the Mogollon Rim, through places with names like Clay Springs, Young, Pumpkin Center, Pinetop.

The final stretch led through the Mazatzal Mountains to Sunflower, and right into downtown Phoenix on Arizona State Road 87, known as the Beeline Highway. Oh, did I mention? Jessica the dog went along too. When Phoenix traffic got too heavy, and Jessica had a couple of near-misses, friends came out with a horse trailer for the final few miles.

After their winter stay near Phoenix, they reversed course back to New

Mexico, and repeated the roundtrip over several years. Elena writes: "Once, we had the heiress to the Quaker Oats fortune pay us to come along for a few weeks. Another time, it rained on us seven straight days. The idea of a wagon came about because our dog, Jessie, was getting too old to keep up." What a life!

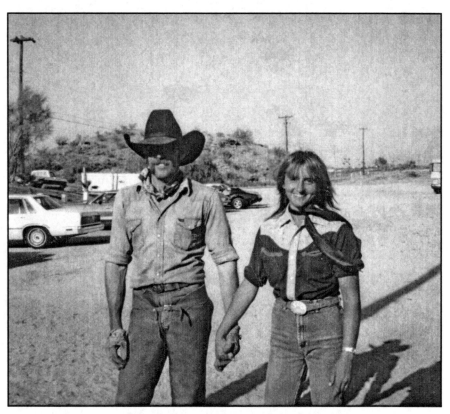

John and Elena Marshall, ready for the trail!

About her book idea. What did I know of that might help? A friend, retired Texas Ranger Joaquin Jackson, of Alpine, Texas, came to mind. His book, "One Ranger - A Memoir", is one of the best-selling books ever published by the University of Texas Press. After 27 years of service, Ranger Jackson became disenchanted with the politics of then-Texas Governor Ann Richards, and the effect of those politics on his

job. In 1993, as a form of protest, he rode his horse more than 400 miles from Alpine to Austin to turn in his badge.

He could offer better advice, so I've gotten them in touch and am eager to see what develops. At the least, they can talk about saddle sores.

God blesses us when we learn about people who've led such extraordinary lives and a book about the Marshalls' experiences would be welcome on my shelf, next to "One Ranger". If you haven't read that, find it and do so. It's readily available on Amazon.com and from book stores.

And next time you're through Socorro, drop into K-Bob's and wish Elena good luck, will you? Order steak, though, and don't be messing around with my shrimp.

46

Where You Are, There Let Me Stay

December 2013

Native American folklore contains fascinating stories. Those of the Mescalero Apache would certainly catch our attention, they being our neighbors to the immediate north.

Recently, I ran across a book titled "American Indian Ghost Stories of the Southwest". The author is Antonio Garcez of Moriarty, New Mexico. The stories within make it seem as if our own Rebecca of The Lodge or Mr. Jenkins of the Cloudcroft Hotel would enjoy knowing their supernatural friends who may exist close by.

You may find the book by either the title or the writer's name on Amazon.com, just one source. One of Mr. Garcez' grandparents was a Mescalero Apache, a storyteller who told these tales to his grandson who was then just a little boy.

Though it may have occurred over a 100 year period, Native Americans across our continent suffered identical fates, being dispossessed of their lands. The westward advance of so many white men and their technologies saw to that.

Since 2009, I've become familiar with legends of the Speckled Trout tribe in upper New York State. Their ancestral home was near the present location of Cooperstown, New York, which isn't far from Albany, the state capital. The presence of colonists and early settlers hastened their demise.

The American Indian Chief Schenevus was the great leader of the Speckled Trout. Based on stories passed down by generations of Indians and white settlers, doubtless there was either truth to the tales told about them or a massive conspiracy to deceive, and I believe the former.

The information I've heard isn't a part of recorded history, per se. Cooperstown is in Otsego County. A book, "The History of Otsego County", written in the late 1880s, doesn't mention the Speckled Trout. Yet a hundred years before, in the late 1700s, the name of a small settlement named Jacksonboro was replaced with the name Schenevus.

Here are some key stories. Chief Schenevus had four sons and three daughters. The girls were Manaho, Otego, and Oneonta. Manaho loved a brave, Manitee, and had often told him, "Where you are, there let me stay". But a chieftain's beautiful daughter was a real catch and Ghangu, a rival of Manitee for Manaho's love, came along one day and pushed Manitee over a cliff.

Manaho found his body at the bottom of Manaho Gorge, which bears that name now but didn't just then. It was called that beginning shortly after Manaho went to the top of the gorge and plunged to death beside her beloved, rather than give in to a life with a pushy fellow like Ghangu.

Even an Indian chieftain could be partial and after the death of his favorite daughter, Manaho, Chief Schenevus aged rapidly, and also became partially blind. He could no longer be a great hunter or effectively lead his people in council. So one day, unable to keep up with his

braves, he called his four sons together and gave them an order. In the way of his time, he was shamed by his waning strength.

"My sons," he said, "I am very old and weary, and I can no longer take part in the hunt or lead the war councils. I would rather die the warrior of my tribe than live my full life old, blind and the object of scorn and pity. Therefore, my sons, I command that your last act of obedience be the slaying of your own father."

The sons didn't dare disobey, so helped their father mount his faithful horse. Chief Schenevus had them follow him to the nearby hunting grounds and aim their arrows at him as they would toward a deer. "I will fall as a slain deer and none of you will bear the shame of my death. This is my last command. I have spoken."

But the great power of the Speckled Trout was gone forever, after the death of their great chief. The continuing settlement of the area finished up what the slaying did not.

Murals, created in 1943 by an artist named Ramsey, though, continue to exist in Schenevus at today's Chief Schenevus Restaurant & Bakery at 56 Main Street. Back in 1990, the murals, flaking and peeling away, were restored by a Fultonham, New York, artist, Debbie Krol, and today they remain very beautiful.

How do I know? That coffee shop and bakery is a favorite place visited yearly, as I return to the area to see the family of Deputy Sheriff Bob Hedman, Jr. His mother and brothers live nearby. Bob ate there as a youth, and looked at those same murals. Bob, as you know, died on December 18, 2004, five miles east of Cloudcroft. Incredible, isn't it, that nine years have passed.

Incidentally, the high school from which Bob graduated, a part of the Schenevus Central School District, is just two blocks from the cafe. His mother worked in the school's cafeteria for years and I've met

with members of the staff who fondly remember a teenaged Bobby Hedman, Jr.

I promised Bob's family I'd visit their home annually and beginning in 2009, have kept my word. It's a long trip so each finds me taking an excursion to another place in the area. Among them, so far: Niagara Falls; Howe Caverns near Albany; the U. S. Military Academy at West Point; Winter Harbor, Maine; the Norman Rockwell Museum near Pittsfield, Massachusetts; and one New York favorite where we watch fresh apples pressed into as fresh an apple juice as you can get, Fly Creek Orchards.

This year's extracurricular activity? Weather permitting, Bob's brothers and I will take four wheelers and ride out to Manaho Gorge, just east of Schenevus. We'll stand at both top and bottom where centuries-old legend has it that Manaho fulfilled her vow to Manitee:

"Where you are, there let me stay."

May God bless the Hedman family this Christmas season and let them understand we appreciate his standing up for the citizens of Otero County, New Mexico.

47

A New Year, A New Path, A New Beginning

January 2014

Here's a foolproof formula for your New Year's resolutions: G + YA + WP = S.

G is for your Goal.

YA, Your Advantages. Stir them in. You're not starting from scratch. There's the support of family and friends and most likely, community. Under family, if you're lucky, there's someone who loves and champions you. If you've so chosen, a church family to boot. Some money, a bank account, and the ability to manage your own finances. A cell phone, a computer, and you know the technology.

You're in control, or think so. You have a key to a door, and can open it freely, in both directions. An understanding of today's trends, access to today's news, what's popular. A driver's license and some kind of vehicle to get around with. Medical insurance or a means of getting necessary care. Prescription medications, but no addiction, nothing illegal. The

pet you love isn't a monkey on your back. You have adequate clothing. You probably already have a job you can keep until you find a better one.

With these advantages, you have a real head start on your 2014 resolutions. Toss in WP, the final ingredient, which only you can provide. Will Power. With all this, you'll get 'er done. The S is for Success.

But suppose your circumstances are different. You're in the Penitentiary of New Mexico at Santa Fe, Level VI, Maximum Security. You're completing a five year sentence for drug usage and robbery. You robbed a gas station for money to buy drugs. You got away. All of five blocks before you got caught. You were so stoned you don't even remember being arrested.

Notice how big the third paragraph is above, the YA? Guess what. About 90% of it just went away. God knows, your New Year's resolution is to live whatever a normal life is and be whatever a good person is. But can you do it?

You're in a six by 10 foot concrete cell, with an open toilet. You have an hour out daily for exercise but it happens maybe four times a week. During hot July, you didn't leave your cell for 24 straight days because of trouble in another building, not your own. You got a shower every six days.

You only see the correction officers guarding you, not helping you correct much that's wrong with your life. Rehabilitation? Really, now.

Your health, largely ignored before prison, has gone downhill. Your teeth are bad from the methamphetamine you used. The one that anchors your bottom plate has a bad cavity. You're number 84 on the list for the dentist, who comes in bi-weekly and treats five patients. You're not Einstein, but this math you can do.

Your right foot has a mysterious infection, common in prisons. Yet another Physician's Assistant, the one familiar with your history, just left for a better job. The beans, rice and potatoes you eat daily, though you like each, have added the wrong kind of weight.

A buddy had the same catheter inserted for 10 months. He bled from infection. His nitroglycerine tablets for a heart condition weren't always brought on time. One day, he laid unconscious on the cell floor for five hours. Those of us within 30 feet had no clue. He could have easily died. Other friends have and it didn't make the news.

For five years, you haven't paid a bill or had a credit card or a checking account, or an income to manage save the six cents per hour you get for mopping. You haven't opened a door with a key, or gone anywhere unescorted, unshackled. You received three letters your first year, one the second, none since. Your daughter from Roswell, who didn't have the money to spare, tried to visit once, but a last minute lockdown turned her away at the gate. She hasn't been back.

On Veterans Day, though you served honorably in the Army or Air Force or Navy or Marines or Coast Guard, your service was completely ignored.

Parole? You've had to prove you had a place outside before you could be paroled, and there was no one to help. So the half-way house was the only alternative. You know the rules are very strict, and you know lots of guys who've come back from there.

Friends have even refused parole, served out their entire sentence, because they know they can't do it. You remember Benny, who was back in two weeks. He suffered the standard fate. Leaving with one set of civilian clothing and $50 and a bus ticket to Albuquerque, he spent $25 on one good meal, had $25 left. His choice: Another meal or some street drugs? Too tempting. He opted for the latter, peed dirty, and was returned, just like that.

You know that two-thirds of those released come back. You think it's really closer to 80%. You know that many who don't return have died.

The job training classes you took were very old, grainy videos, no "hands on". Instructors with hair from the 70s, bellbottoms. What work can you do? For sure it'll be minimum wage, bottom of the food chain. "He's the con," they'll whisper.

Theoretical situations? During 2006, in an incredible experience, I spent 10 months in Santa Fe's maximum security prison. The stories above are real stories I saw of people like Benny, Bob, Chris, Danny, Ernie, Martin, Raul, Richard, and Sam, who became friends. Some are still there. Some are dead.

Is there anyone or anyplace that will help them with the advantages you have in paragraph three?

My good friend Chris Cleveland, a fellow inmate for months, will. He's formed New Path Ministries. Sometimes I visit him and his dad and his son in Albuquerque. Chris is dedicated to bringing the Bennys and Sams and Rauls back to society in an orderly way. In his words:

"We are a nonprofit Christian organization that is dedicated to helping the hard-cord drug addict, alcoholic, and those with life-controlling problems. Our program involves a minimum six month commitment. The men are in a group live-in environment.

They are taught a disciplined life-style and are very much involved in Christian activity. They're helped to change their behavior pattern with personal and group training covering drug-alcohol abuse. We work with them in the principles of Christianity, producing people who are able to function in our society as Christian citizens. Through daily spiritual encouragement and Bible studies, we are able to instill within the individual a sense of personal conviction, dignity, and responsibility not only toward himself, but toward society as a whole. Thank you for your support."

Chris Cleveland, right center with a hearty laugh, with his New Path group during 2014.

New Path is located at 511 Madeira SE, Albuquerque NM 87108. There's room for 13 men and the facility is full. Five are former inmates. There's always a waiting list. You can write Chris there or call him at 505-991-6388. Learn more at www.newpathministries.org . I pray for Chris and have helped him financially for several years. Maybe you'll assist someone in a new beginning.

Chris has no illusions about prison. "It's a home they earned. There is no hope. There is only darkness. But there can be redemption. If you decide to help, you will never look at jail or prison in the same way again."

48

A Classic Cloudcroft Confrontation: Little Angel vs. Little Devil

March 2014

Hollywood producer, director and actor Ash Adams now owns a little piece of Cloudcroft, New Mexico. It's a 1952 Spartan Royal Spartanette travel trailer, 35 feet long. Ownership didn't come easily.

I like to see old things restored and appreciated. My Sacramento Mountains neighbor inherited the Spartanette and brought it from Colorado three years ago. It had languished on his property since.

Languishment bothers me, since mice and skunks take advantage, so I acquired the vintage trailer. My plans were uncertain, though noble.

Comparing sands in the hourglass to projects waiting, there's a mismatch, so reluctantly I listed it on eBay. Spartanettes, manufactured in Oklahoma after WWII by the Spartan Aircraft Company, are quality and highly collectible. This one, though not pristine, was an ideal restoration candidate.

I've done eBay business 12+ years, with a 100% positive feedback rating over hundreds of transactions, large and small. The listing ended January 27th. The winning bidder was from California. I stood to make a decent profit, and was content.

Within one hour, he called, crying. "Why did I bid? I already have four and room for no more. My wife will kill me. What was I thinking? I can't do this," he said. He'd sounded intoxicated. Well, this is going well, I thought. Stiffed by the auction winner. The Little Devil who lives on my left shoulder smiled triumphantly, cynically.

Want to be a skeptic? Be a cop for more than 30 years, watch human nature at work. That'll do it. But a Little Angel stands on my right shoulder, placed by my mother to keep watch, years ago. "Do the right thing, and you'll be all right," said my ma, who died in 2008. She'd visited Cloudcroft in 1996, and luckily for me, scattered Little Angel dust around.

Three other bidders were within $100 each. Ash Adams, the runner-up, had a "zero" eBay tally. He'd joined just to bid on the trailer. The Little Devil said: "Skip him, go to the next guy with the proven record." The persistent Little Angel said: "Do the right thing…" Okay, okay.

It was another classic case of good vs. evil, Angel vs. Devil.

Ash accepted my Second Chance offer, and we had a contract. A $200 deposit was required within 24 hours. It was made, although late. Full payment was due within seven days, February 3rd. As of today, February 20th, I haven't actually received it yet. Forty-five phone calls and numerous e-mails have transpired. I've gotten a thousand bucks. All along the smug Little Devil said: "Told you so."

Ash remarked early on: "In Hollywood, trust is a four letter word that starts with an 'F'." Ash produced and starred in a movie called "Once Fallen", also starring Ed Harris, Amy Madigan, Brian Presley, and Alison Eastwood, Dirty Harry's daughter. An earlier effort was: "I Spit on Your

Grave". A work in progress is "White Cargo". Ash turned 50 during the Spartanette sales saga, on February 7, 2014. He'll live in it, in Malibu.

Ash's friend, Brian, not the actor above, handles financial details along with Ash's father, a California attorney. Late in the game, Ash wanted to hold final payment until his retrieval crew, Charles and Lis, saw the trailer on Saturday, February 8th. By then I had the thousand deposit. The cost to tow it would be another $2500. With the buyer having invested that much, I disregarded the Little Devil and listened to the Little Angel.

Really, I wanted Ash to come to Cloudcroft personally so he'd make a movie here. To see us is to love us. But okay, okay. Send Charles and Lis.

"How do I know there is a trailer, that this isn't a complete fabrication?" asked Ash, invoking his Hollywood definition of trust. "I am not a crook!" I exclaimed, in my best Richard Nixon imitation, hoping to sell the Spartanette and win a part in a movie, too. It didn't work. Final payment was delayed well beyond the seven days.

Lis and Charles arrived at midnight Friday, February 7th, missing Ash's birthday party. They stayed at the Summit Inn, Judge Ron Todd's place, and were happy. "We considered The Lodge," said Lis, "but I'm afraid of ghosts." I assured her that Rebecca is very friendly.

I wouldn't let the trailer leave with old tires, so we headed for Alamogordo early Saturday. From the trestle, Lis was fascinated with the view of White Sands. "What's that, water?" she asked. Don't you hate to have first time visitors and not give them the nickel tour?

At the tire store, I could pay and receive a discount for military service and add the cost of tires to the total, or let Charles/Lis spend an extra fifty bucks. The Little Devil stood his skeptical ground. I wavered, but listened to the Little Angel. Out came my credit card, up went the bill due another $453 dollars. Somewhere my mother was smiling. The skeptic/cynic in me stirred uneasily.

We ate at IHOP while tires were installed. Lis/Charles told me about their two teenage sons, the challenge of rearing them. "Oh sure," said the Little Devil. Our food was served. "Mind if we pray?" asked Charles. The Little Angel beamed! The scale tipped towards trust, the five letter version starting with a "T".

We worked frantically on Saturday, February 8th, installing tires/wheels/trailer lighting. Charles/Lis had left their children with friends and were pressed, eager to leave. OCSO Deputy Wes Green dropped by, got caught up in tire changing and the like. "What kind of community is this?" asked Charles. "You'll never see a Los Angeles cop do that." You don't know the half of it, I thought, smiling.

At 4 PM, we were ready. Charles telephoned Brian/Ash to make the final payment via Paypal. They did. Paypal immediately placed a four-day hold on clearance of the funds. "Don't ship the property until this is cleared," said Paypal. The Little Devil swaggered in triumph. Decision time. Who do you trust? The Little Angel looked me square in the eyes. "Remember the breakfast prayer," she said.

The 1952 Spartanette, resting near Mayhill, ready to roll to California!

"Be safe, God bless!" I said to Charles/Lis, watching as my collateral rolled away, towards the land of Make Believe. I'd insisted they take Highway 244 to Highway 70, then west, for safety's sake. They called three times en route, arriving home in one piece.

Final payment of a few thousand? Not yet. A conference call with Paypal and the buyer's agent last night, February 19th, assured me it has been made, is in a holding pattern, and would be deposited to my account by Monday, February 24th. Ash's new saga, "Sale of the Spartanette", is playing out as promised. Forgive me – Ash, Brian, Charles and Lis – for my cynical ways.

Score one for the Little Angel and trust. Ahhh, the power of prayer! Try it sometime, you'll like it. And thanks again, ma.

49

The Night Johnny Lost Sue on U. S. Highway 82

May 2014

Amazing or amusing? You decide.

Last month, I said that to write of actual law enforcement events encountered in the Sacramentos was difficult, but there are cases that involve "strangers passing through" that might be mentioned.

The facts of this case are true, but names and places have been fictionalized. Let's talk about Johnny from Caarswell. Yes, one of our familiar cities to the east.

Johnny owned a restaurant in his hometown, and apparently was well known. In 1999, he invited a divorced third-grade school teacher, the mother of a little girl, on a weekend date to Ruidoso, and she accepted. We'll call her Sue.

Sue found a babysitter, and on Friday afternoon, she and Johnny set out for Ruidoso. They encountered standstill traffic while westbound on U. S. 70 near Hondo, the result of a fatality accident ahead.

Johnny had a serious supply of booze in his car. He also had a loaded 9 mm pistol. I'm not sure what housing arrangements had been made, but it was a first date and much later, having spoken to Sue, I believed her expectations for the weekend were far lower on the "Wild & Crazy" meter than were Johnny's.

Johnny generously partook of the booze – hard stuff – en route, and while stopped on Highway 70. Sue sipped but maintained her cool.

Tired of waiting for the highway to open, Johnny retraced his route, took Highway 13 to U. S. 82, and was headed for Highway 244 and over to Ruidoso that way. You're familiar with all those roads.

It was the "long way around" but hey…a pretty girl at your side…all the booze anyone could want…a loaded gun with which to defend yourself…a long weekend ahead. What the heck!

Enter one each Otero County deputy Y. T. Anders, Yours Truly, on patrol eastbound between Cloudcroft and Mayhill. I drove by a car stopped partially in the driving lane on the westbound side, the engine running, a male behind the driver's wheel. Johnny. It wasn't late but it was dark.

Best guess before stopping? Car trouble. As I'd driven by, I only saw the one person. I drove back, pulled up behind the vehicle, and turned on my red lights since we were in a curve, in the roadway, in the dark.

I radioed in the stop. Sgt Jeff Farmer wasn't too far away and started to the location. I walked to the driver's door, where it was immediately apparent that Johnny was like a well-burnt piece of bread. Toasted.

Johnny, a real piece of work, quickly became belligerent. Among his accusations…"You scared her!" he yelled. Scared who? "My girlfriend had to pee and now she won't come out of the woods! She's afraid of you! Leave us alone so she'll come back!!"

Well…there were two "little red cups" in Johnny's car, complete with booze, but a key woman's ingredient was missing, a purse. There was a small bag of women's clothing.

Sue seemed to be taking a long time in the woods and wouldn't return to the car. Jeff Farmer had arrived and we did everything possible to coax even a scared person back. Johnny had been alone when I arrived and I'd seen or heard no one else, but we were concerned for the missing woman. Perhaps she was intoxicated, and was fearful of being arrested. Johnny could only yell and scream when asked if she'd taken her purse when she left. She'd had to cross a barbed-wire fence on the bank at the roadway's edge.

I frisked the car for our safety and found the fully loaded 9 mm under Johnny's seat, along with an ample supply of an open container of booze, and more capped at the ready. Jeff and I continued to encourage Sue to return from the woods, no luck. Jeff drove a couple of miles in each direction, no success there either.

I arrested Johnny for DWI and possession of a firearm while intoxicated. He was not a happy camper, and continued to vehemently accuse us of having put his girlfriend in danger by having scared her.

I did the usual required legal things involved in such an arrest. When told he'd appear before a magistrate in Otero County, Johnny insisted on appearing before Judge Buford T. Injustice of Caarswell instead, and repeatedly demanded to see him. It was apparent they were buds in some way.

Johnny was placed into jail. The "woman in the woods" continued to bother me, and as soon as possible, I returned to the scene and searched for her again. Somehow I'd gathered enough information to call the Caarswell police who found her at home around 3 AM. By 4 AM, I'd talked to Sue by telephone.

She was an extremely nice – sober – common sensical – educated – young woman, who said that as the evening had worn on and the roundabout trip took place, Johnny had become sexually aggressive, drunk, and obnoxious to the point she'd begun to worry about her personal safety. "What really scared me, Deputy Anders," she said, "was wondering how my daughter would fare without me if it came to that."

She finally decided that the "need to pee" excuse was her only hope of getting away from Johnny. Convincing him to stop, she took her purse, climbed the fence, went far back into the woods, turned east towards home, and walked perhaps two miles before risking returning to Highway 82. She tried hitchhiking and an 18 wheeler picked her up and took her to her hometown and safety. It would be her first and last date with Johnny, Sue said. She'd never seen my police vehicle or any red lights.

A couple of months went by and I heard nothing about the case. The usual subpoenas were missing. Inquiring in the proper place, and asking again over perhaps six months or a year, no record could ever be found, though I had all my paperwork including the case number. Apparently Johnny and Judge Injustice really were good friends, and my guess is that some favors were called in.

During the first few years of my career, I found such events amazing. By 1999 and at the 25 year point, I found them more amusing, in a frustrating way. The truth is, we live in an imperfect world, because it's composed of human beings.

When I drive through Caarswell now, I see Johnny's café, closed and empty for a long time. Most often, what goes around comes around, and the law of averages tells me it's all worked out.

I hope Sue met the right guy. Her daughter is probably a college student now, and I'm glad Sue got home safely in 1999 to help her little girl grow up.

50

Some Secrets of the Sacramentos

June 2014

You live comfortably in your house or cabin, surrounded by 500,000 acres of national forest. You get around mostly on paved roads. There are some things that Lady Lincoln, the matriarch of the woods, doesn't tell you about. There are secrets in the Sacramento Mountains.

One of them? The homeless who occupy these lands. They're most often greeted by law enforcement, the deputy summoned by someone who lives close to where squatters have settled. The citizen who called isn't always reporting what has happened, but is fearful of what might happen.

The homeless are usually men. But not always. Here are some I met who lived in tents or cars, due to their circumstances. If this is a problem, it's a problem that has parallels to the flowers in your mountain garden. Just as the winters only allow your flowers to be annuals, not perennials, it's like that with the homeless.

They arrive in the spring, after nighttime temperatures have risen to a tolerable level. They leave in the fall, when temperatures have fallen to

less than that tolerable level. Where they go is anyone's guess – some-one else's secret – but all of mankind is tuned in to survival, so they find a place.

At the very upper end of Wills Canyon, a large orange tent was aban-doned after a summer. It hadn't been a hunter's camp. Evidence sug-gested a lengthy stay. Who'd been there? We never found out.

Have you hiked the OSHA trail? If so, you hiked within a quarter mile of a similar "permanent" camp, a brush and pole-covered tent structure which still exists after several years, though falling down. When you walk the trail, it's out of sight over a small mountain top, well hidden.

A young woman, a poet, lived in Cloudcroft years ago, managed cabins for a year. She was beautiful, a free spirit, about 30. She went away for another year, but returned with a boyfriend. They lived in a tent on Little Heliport Road for a complete summer. The Forest Service only allows occupation of a campsite for two weeks, but it's simple enough to move a few hundred feet up or down the road. When she left, where did she go? I couldn't tell you. I wonder about her.

Often the homeless are in an older car or truck that has mechanical problems. On Carr Canyon Road, just east of Mayhill, a man driving a very early model Ford Taurus parked about a mile north of U. S. Highway 82. The road makes a sharp turn to the left there at a wide spot, a place where his car ran out of transmission fluid, where he settled. It was a dusty place, not a good place to stay, but to him, it was home. He was there a few weeks.

People who lived up that road worried he might take things, so they called. I responded, and as usual, checked him for wants or warrants. It's always possible the person is wanted for criminal acts, or that some-one has reported him or her missing. As is often the case, neither situ-ation applied. The initial discussion wasn't pleasant, as a person who

knows that he or she isn't wanted or sought resents being checked on, and that's understandable.

This man wouldn't have done well as a Walmart greeter. He was a camper but not a happy one, but we got through that phase. Neighbors who lived in regular homes nearby continued to be alarmed by his presence, continued to call the Sheriff's Office. He wasn't breaking any law. How could I solve the situation? His destination lay east. Larger towns like Artesia, Carlsbad, or Roswell could provide more in the way of assistance.

I decided to go back armed to the teeth. "How many quarts of transmission fluid would it take to get you to Artesia?" I asked. His calculation was six, so I went back fully armed with eight quarts, purchased at Allsup's. He left eastbound, the car trailing smoke. I never saw him again, nor did the Otero County citizens who'd called. It's not good to transfer your problems, but there didn't seem to be a better alternative.

A homeless man drifted into town, and homesteaded in the hallway of the Cloudcroft Hotel mall. Well-meaning persons there "took him in", and he gladly accepted their generosity, but became more and more demanding, until finally persuaded to move on. He was more of an issue for the Cloudcroft Police.

An attractive, bright woman in her 40s lived in her car on Benson Ridge Road, a few miles toward Sunspot off the Sunspot Highway, for several months. She'd been an investigative reporter for an area newspaper, and wrote well. I remember reading her work. She'd lost her job due to a staff cutback. She was proud, not accustomed to seeking help beyond her own resources, and didn't want assistance. Her car ran, but she had few funds with which to operate it.

Where did she get water? How did she bathe? How did she obtain food? Lady Lincoln might know those answers, but I don't. I talked to the woman a few times, provided a few basic necessities. In the fall,

she moved on. Where? Who knows. She was another of those annual forest flowers.

I remember that the Cloudcroft ministerial alliance often provided help in such situations, and that Mrs. Gloria Blakey frequently discounted a room at the Buckhorn Cabins to assist. Again, thank you!

The growing, changing, seasonal nature of the forest and the land covers up places, which become secret places. The roadbed of the Cloud Climbing Railroad is one. There's still evidence of the railroad, but it's often buried. If you recognize a portion of the roadbed, you can dig just a few inches below the surface and find numerous artifacts. One example – spikes by the tens and hundreds, actually. If you're not tuned in to where you're walking, you'll happily skip over them, unaware of their presence. Meanwhile, the forest is consuming them.

Where the homeless lady poet lived? Within 300 feet of her former campsite, an airplane – a Cessna 172 – crashed with four souls aboard, more than 10 years ago. The aircraft was totally destroyed, but miraculously, everyone survived. Doug Huntsucker, who owned the Aspen Café and was target shooting nearby, was the first to reach those folks. Today, if you know where to look, one sheared-off tree trunk remains, but otherwise nothing marks the spot.

Once again, the wise old woods gods have purified their turf, and managed to create yet another secret. In the secretive Sacramentos.

51

In New Mexico, These Are a Few of My Favorite Things

July 2014

Working for more than 50 years, as many of you probably did or will, it came as a shock to learn my former employer was happy to just send me a check and have me stay home. There's a message in there some-where. But believe me - one quickly adjusts.

Maybe it's why so many young Americans are lazy. If they'd had this program when I was 20, I'd have signed on.

Travel is now a favorite activity, and I do my best to take advantage. A short trip to Knoxville, Tennessee, took place last week. The cost of gasoline, though, gives one serious purchase. What are some places closer to home – generally reachable on one tank of fuel – that are my favorite places, places I recommend you visit?

I'm no travel guide and won't attempt to tell you step-by-step how to reach these. There are plenty of maps and there's GPS, and the Internet via Google provides adequate information on that aspect.

Locally, don't miss a little day trip to Hornbuckle Hill. It's just above Timberon, to the west, on a good road. On a clear day, you can see to El Paso. See a photo at www.panoramio.com/photo/19024889. The ghost of Simeon Hournbuckle, who homesteaded there and walked sheep up and down the mountains, probably won't be upset with you personally for the misspelling. Take water and a lunch.

Also right here close at home are Bluff Springs, the trip up Prestridge Hill into Hay Canyon, and a longer drive to Dell City just across the Texas border, below Weed and Pinion.

The Dell City trip will be an all-day affair, and make sure you have a good spare and the equipment and ability to change a flat. Two spares are better. Take along water and snacks, your GPS, cell phone, and a good map. As a deputy, before GPS days, I took a good compass. Have lunch at a little café in Dell City. If the trip down wears on you, drive into El Paso and come home that way. Not a problem. You'll experience the beauty of Cornucopia Draw, perhaps see an eagle, and appreciate the vastness of Otero Mesa.

Successful completion of the Dell City trip qualifies you to try the Westside Road drive from U. S. Highway 82 in High Rolls around the mountain rim, which takes you through Hornbuckle Hill and back up the Timberon Road into Cloudcroft via Sunspot. About a four to five hour venture, again with spares/water/lunch…and common sense. Watch the weather, and telephone the Sheriff's Office beforehand to ask if there's any known road problems. That also alerts them that you're out there. You might also telephone when you successfully complete your trip.

Ah, White Sands National Monument, not to be missed! One of only two places like it in the world, and the other is in Africa. Sign up online for one of the monthly trips to Lake Lucero, source of the sand which isn't sand but gypsum. Check the schedule – Lake Lucero trips

are suspended during the summer. You'll meet a ranger at the Small Missile Range Gate, 25 miles west of White Sands, for that tour.

I've always wondered…is that a range for small missiles or a small range for intermediate and large missiles?

Got time to head to the northern part of our state? A favorite trip a few years back took me from Raton to Shiprock, just south of the Colorado border, on U. S. 64. This led through Cimarron, then around "the loop" to Red River, Questa, San Cristobal, Taos, Angel Fire, and Eagle Nest. Wheeler Peak, at 13,161 feet the highest in New Mexico, is on that route.

I took a canoe and paddled the Rio Grande below Taos. If water level is sufficient, you can rent one or do a raft trip. And yes, it's the same Rio Grande which flows between El Paso and Juarez.

Leaving Taos, you'll continue to Tres Piedras and Tierra Amarilla. No one in Cloudcroft who was at the Cloudcroft High School football playoff game in 2002 – Cody Adams was our quarterback - will ever forget Tierra Amarilla. It was a very cold day. We won, advancing to the state finals.

The folks in that area are descendants of Spaniards and not from Mexico and you should know that. Learn how they took over the courthouse back in the 1960s, a fascinating story not well publicized in museums in Albuquerque and Santa Fe.

Continuing west on U. S. 64 takes you to Chama, home of the world's highest and longest working steam train and scenic railway, the Cumbres & Toltec. My wife and I just finished our second annual volunteer work project there, June 23 -27. Take the train ride which weaves in and out of Colorado, ends at Antonito. Take my word for this – the lunch at Osier, Colorado, is worth the cost. Look at www. coloradonewmexicosteamtrain.org and click on Web Cams for two

live shots of the Chama train yard. Last week, we would have waved to you!

Continue into Dulce, Farmington, and Shiprock. Along the way, visit Navajo Lake, the Aztec Ruins National Monument, and the Salmon Ruins. Return to Albuquerque via U. S. Highway 550 from Bloomfield. Drive across 30 miles of (usually) good dirt road to Chaco Canyon National Park, and try to figure out what possessed early Native Americans to live there a few thousand years ago.

Watch the weather on the drive to Chaco Canyon, there's a low spot in the middle of that drive and a thunderstorm almost kept me on the wrong side of the arroyo. Back on U. S. 550, through Cuba, stop at Jemez Springs on State Highway 126 and boil like a lobster in a hot bath, and get a massage. Life doesn't get much better! Highway 550 will soon return you to Interstate 25.

Coming or going, a stop at the Three Rivers Petroglyph Site, 17 miles north of Tularosa on U. S. Highway 54, gives you up close and personal access to more than 21,000 rock drawings. Some folks claim it's the best thing to see in New Mexico! Take water and snacks, and pay just a small fee per carload to visit. Check out the great Three Rivers store at the turnoff, and the 1904 schoolhouse just behind it, too.

Take someone you care about on these trips and they're even better. Stop into a little church along the way on Sunday mornings where you're always welcome and that will add to your conviction that we're blessed to live in New Mexico!

52

Thanksgiving – A Time to Remember Health Care Workers

November 2014

When we're saying our Thanksgiving prayers this month, health care workers should be high on our list.

As a sheriff's deputy in the Sacramento Mountains, I was always grateful for our EMS volunteers. They do a critical job and daily put themselves in harm's way as they encounter various medical conditions.

My daughter, who graduated from Cloudcroft High School in 2002, was a pretty fair athlete but had serious asthma problems. We had some scary close calls as our EMS folks rushed her "down the hill" and I thank God for them. I am eternally grateful.

Anyone who deals with the ill or injured falls into my "thanks for them" category. That includes the staff at the Sacramento Mountain Medical Clinic and the health care givers in Alamogordo. They never know what they'll be exposed to daily.

As deputies, we were issued rudimentary gear for our protection, items which included rubber gloves, face masks, and containers for items like bloody syringes. It wasn't easy to put on safety equipment during events which developed quickly, or when immediate action was needed on arrival, such as extricating someone from a vehicle accident where fire might be imminent.

Another factor - we dealt with friends and neighbors, and it almost seemed we were saying: "You're not clean enough for me!" if you donned such gear, and I just couldn't always do it. So I/we took our chances. What were some of the dangerous medical situations we met? Exposure to AIDS and hepatitis were just two.

During the 1990s in San Antonio, Texas, one of my young officers was searching a Volkswagen Bug for evidence after a DWI arrest. Roger was a fine young man, with a wife and small child. He ran his hand under a car seat, and punctured a finger on a bloody syringe. The person in custody, oddly, was a Medal of Honor recipient, a real hero who'd jumped on a grenade in Vietnam to save fellow soldiers. It was a miracle he hadn't been killed. He was a patient for more than two years and became addicted to pain killers, and later heroin.

He voluntarily took me to his home and produced medical records which revealed he'd had Dengue Fever, so we had information to give to the hospital for the officer's benefit. Roger was treated successfully. He was one of many I knew who were exposed to such danger.

Prior to Air Force active duty, I began my professional work career after college as the assistant personnel director of a 600 bed hospital in Baton Rouge, Louisiana, and thus began my affinity for those in health care.

All the problems I've known of personally seem to pale in comparison to today's challenge to contain Ebola.

It's funny the effects such an outbreak can have on those of us remote from it. For putting up with the craziness of my law enforcement career without complaint, I promised my wife she could take an annual trip with good friends, and they've steadily crossed places like Tanzania in Africa; Ecuador; Costa Rica; and various sites in our own country off their bucket list.

The 20 year dream of the group's leader has been a safari trip to see gorillas in Uganda and Rwanda in Central Africa. For the past 17 months, hard work made this a potential reality. Each person invested just under $10,000 in fees, government permits, and airline tickets. No one in the group is wealthy and it has been a serious commitment, one saved for.

As you're guessing, the bucket developed Ebola-related leaks and reluctantly, the trip has finally been cancelled, officially postponed. Just too many uncertains for comfort. I write this on October 18th. They were to leave tomorrow.

The ladies purchased trip insurance but it doesn't cover this. The safari company has issued a voucher good for a year for their $5300 portion but I believe we've only seen the tip of the iceberg with Ebola, a Titanic-sized berg that probably won't even begin to melt in 12 months.

I've watched the last few weeks as the excitement level of the Gorilla Girls rose – while calls to such agencies as the federal Center for Disease Control increased, only to receive stone-walling non-answers (after all, it's a federal agency, with an appointed director, etc.) – as the final realization set in that no one's life was worth $10,000 and that tomorrow is another day…and that we have to be grateful that their only loss is money, sometimes a minor issue in the scheme of things.

The truth is – if you have your health – anything is possible; and without it, not much else really matters. The World Health Organization

says that in West Africa, those affected by Ebola will perish at the rate of 70%. They're the folks with the real problems.

I have no claim to any heroics in health care, but please allow me to salute a forbearer who gave his all to the United States and his fellow man in such a cause.

As a young boy, I listened to stories about my Grandfather Anders' younger brother, John, who'd perished as a young man while treating the sick. My predecessors were farmers – ranchers – dairymen – carpenters – mechanics – railroad men. But my Great Uncle John graduated from medical school, an unusual thing in our rural family. My guess was he'd contracted smallpox or typhoid. I didn't even know where he was buried.

Passing a cemetery named Roseland in a small Mississippi town two years ago, making a left turn I've probably made a hundred times before, my gaze lingered just a second longer on a tombstone that blocked one behind it, and the one previously hidden came into view. I saw: ANDERS. There since 1906 have laid the earthly remains of my Uncle John. I learned he'd passed away in Central America during the building of the Panama Canal, treating malaria victims. He died of malaria, of course. He was just 26.

So God bless people like Uncle John and those of the current era who risk their own health in order to protect the rest of us. This Thanksgiving, God, we commend them to You for their unselfish work, and we pray for the recovery of those who are ill.

Author's note: The Ebola crisis passed and my wife and her group were able to safely travel to Africa and see the mountain gorillas during June 2015. Following is her account. It appeared in the Cloudcroft Mountain Monthly in August 2015.

Trip of a Lifetime? You decide
by Cynthia Anders

I'm retired. So now what? Volunteer at church, the library? Not this adventurer. Since 2010, I have been fortunate enough to holiday in Ecuador, Tanzania, Costa Rica and the National Parks in Utah and Arizona. This year four friends and I chose gorilla tracking in Rwanda and Uganda. Crazy – maybe. Exciting – definitely.

Our adventure began traveling through the beautiful terraced hills of the Parc Nacional des Volcans or the Volcanoes National Park on the Rwanda side. Our luxury lodge was nestled on a hillside overlooking five volcanoes and Lake Kivu. Our first day began at the Park Ranger station where we got specific instructions on hiking and gorilla protocol. We proceeded to the edge of the park entrance after hiking through a village and across several fields of tea, beans and potatoes. Then the fun began. We slugged through forest, stinging nettles, ankle deep mud and rain to reach our 10,000 feet destination. The forest opened up and there was a family of eight gorillas. We were introduced to the oldest living silverback in the world. He is 43 years old, losing teeth and sight but still the ruler of his group. Cameras and iPhones were snapping photos left and right. We were within 4-5 feet of the primates throughout our hour long visit. One of our group was lounging next to a female and got gently touched on the head! "I'm never washing my hair again!!" was her reaction. The guide encouraged her to get up so the gorilla could move to her next resting place. We thought that it couldn't get any better than this. We were wrong.

Did I mention that there was a lot of driving to get to our destinations? Each day saw 2-3 hours of bouncing across rugged mountain roads, so the idea of hiking seemed a respite from the trips. Day two was only a hike to 8400 feet so it would be easy – or so we thought. This route took us straight up, our feet standing precariously on slippery vegetation looking down the side of a steep mountain. Today we saw a female

who had lost a paw to poachers, but this didn't slow her down. She was so adept at grabbing juicy plants, sliding the best parts off the stalk and eating them – it was amazing to watch her. At one point, a silverback that had been above us in the forest decided to let us know who was boss. He bounded down the hillside about 5 feet from us then casually strolled away putting his hind end in our direction. No mistaking his message! Every family has one silverback (sometimes 2 or 3), at least 2-3 females, many juveniles and babies. Occasionally we saw black-backs which are younger males. These males usually leave the family and seek out their own females from other places.

Cynthia, my wife, in Rwanda, Africa, with a silverback gorilla five feet away, June 2015.

Our next excursion took us across the border into Uganda. Border crossings are tedious and take time – usually 1-2 hours. We also had to pay to enter. Ah! The cost of travel. We proceeded to the Bwindi Impenetrable Forest. This ranger station was at the top of the mountain

so the first half of the hike was downhill into a tea plantation and across to the nesting place of the gorillas. We could see them from above. Now here things get exciting. The family had 2 silverbacks, 2 females, 4 juveniles and 2 babies. Our group was snapping away when one of the juveniles decided to pass by. He stopped and sniffed me on the leg, I stepped back and he gracefully passed on as his group moved to find their evening nesting place. I was beside myself! Even the grueling hike out of the forest could not take away the incredible experience of the Mountain Gorilla. Just call me Cynthia Fossey! I'd say this was a trip of a lifetime.

53

A Cloudcroft Christmas Trip

December 2014

There's nothing quite like a Cloudcroft Christmas. And getting here can be almost half the fun.

Rolling in yesterday, it had taken me two weeks to return, having started from the East Coast. What a beautiful country we have!

Traveling on the cheap in my '68 Shasta Compact – it's 12 feet long and I'm over six feet long – my first night was in Crestview, Florida, with nothing but the best in RV parks – the Walmart parking lot. Except there's no extension cord for a heater.

The Shasta was purchased to replace a '56 Shasta "canned ham" for solo travel. I sold the '56 and later regretted it, so a replacement was obtained.

The thermometer that night fell to 28 degrees, and it's possible my body temperature did too. I was one cold duck. What a way to save a buck.

Next stop was Aunt Margie's house in Mississippi. It's where I grew up, and I belong to the local Historical & Genealogical Society. On November 8[th], they sponsored the 150[th] anniversary celebration of the Civil War Battle of Liberty. It was my honor to give a hay wagon tour to five battle sites, and to sell t-shirts. Been there, done that, got the t-shirt. And you thought I rode into town on a turnip truck! It was a hay wagon, big difference.

My aunt is 87; the youngest sibling of my mother's eight, and the only one still living. She's a trip in herself, and we always have great visits. It was good to see her and her dog Queenie. It was really good to sleep in Aunt Margie's warm spare room, with the Shasta left outside.

Her name is really Marjorie and she prefers that, but to me, she's been Aunt Margie since I was just a little guy, and Aunt Margie she remains.

For Veteran's Day, I attended the annual open house of the Camp Van Dorn WWII Military Museum in Centreville, Mississippi. The camp existed only two years during the early 1940s, and was a training facility for units that invaded Europe at Normandy; troops later involved in the Battle of the Bulge. The museum, in an old refurbished bank building, is a quality place.

Southwest Mississippi is "hot" with fracking (not a curse word) oil production from the Tuscaloosa Shale Formation, and one constantly dodges white pickup trucks and larger vehicles involved in such activity. My folks left my sister and me some mineral rights, so I stop and cross my fingers while in the vicinity. So far it hasn't worked.

On to Jasper in East Texas, where I visited my old friend, Lyle, my flying boss in the early 1970s. Best pilot I've ever known. It's always a thrill to drive down the old runway of Piney Woods Airport and remember launching myself from there in Days Gone By. The airstrip is now closed and serves as his driveway.

Next stop was in the countryside near San Antonio, and another Three Dog Night in the Shasta outside a friend's house. I had an extension cord for my little electric heater, but just my luck – the cord, I believe, was too short - and I froze again while Odie, Muggie, and Jane Doe – his three dogs, slept warmly inside on the couch. I vowed to treat myself to an additional heater at the next Walmart.

Feeling sorry for me, huh? Ha ha, gotcha! My wife flew into San Antonio, fresh from the heartbreak of a cancelled trip to Africa to visit gorillas – cancellation due to the Ebola threat – and treated me to four nights on the San Antonio Riverwalk in a luxury hotel. Even my friend's dogs were envious. The little Shasta just waited at his house, cold.

The Christmas lights are always up at Mi Tierra Restaurant in El Mercado – the market – and places like Casa Rio on the Riverwalk beckon. As does one of my favorite little cafes in the world, Tommy's Mexican Food near the close-by courthouse. I didn't get hungry, and I didn't get cold. For four days and nights.

On November 15th, my San Antonio Police cadet class met in Mico, Texas, near Bandera, and celebrated the 40th anniversary of our graduation. Thirty-two of 36 are still kicking, and I donated a bottle of Witherspoon bourbon, made in Lewisville, Texas, for the Last One Standing. Down the road, he or she will drink to the memory of those of us who are no longer standing. Our youngest classmate, Gary, now 60, will be the Keeper of the Bottle, and hopes to remain so.

On towards Cloudcroft! Lum's BBQ – the World's Best! – in Junction, Texas, just a mile off Interstate 10, always draws my attention, and this trip was no different. Highly recommended, and have the brisket.

I know it's the World's Best because it says so on the sign.

Into Ft. Stockton, where, like the wagon trains of yesteryear, I always

restock. My new heater-to-be awaited me at Walmart! Alas, cold weather had beaten me there…and the shelves were bare. So I satisfied myself with a new sleeping bag, to be doubled with the one I already had.

The IH10 RV Park advertised Full Hookups, Hot Showers, and Clean Restrooms. Consider this a review and a warning…let Desperation and no other reason compel you to stop there. Go to Comanche Land next door instead.

My pain, I thought, would be mollified by a breakfast visit to another of the World's Best Eateries, Pepito's, in downtown Ft. Stockton… home of Senor Peppy the Chihuahua, and La Sofia the Cat. And The Beautiful Sonia, cashier and server. But horrors! It was closed!

But then I recalled…last visit, the owner was in a rent dispute and said he was moving to near the Walmart – where I found him, thank the Good Lord for favors. And most excellent Mexican food. That far west on Interstate 10, San Antonio breakfast tacos have transformed themselves into breakfast burritos, but that's okay. Burritos are bigger.

And now I'm here, having survived a final dash through another Land of White Pickups between Stockton and Artesia…the oil patch development is something else. Little Orla is bursting at the seams. The U. S. Highway 285 surface through that area is a mess. A pothole nightmare.

Back in Schulenburg, Texas, between Houston and San Antonio, I'd stopped at the Oakridge Smokehouse. If you think I travel from one good café to another…okay, guilty. The Smokehouse has kick butt buffets. Browsing the gift shop, I'd seen a sign: "The best Christmas gifts are memories." Well, hello.

This year, a Cloudcroft Christmas will be the icing on my memory cake. Nothing better. If you haven't spent the holidays here – the celebration of the birth of our Lord - do it, and do it with family. You'll be glad you did.

54

A Very Humane Thought
for the New Year

January 2015

Another year begins in Cloudcroft. Another year of memories starts to accumulate. May those you gather during 2015 be pleasant ones!

Working as a Sheriff's Deputy, I met many mountain residents and contrary to what you may believe, often those encounters had little or nothing to do with police work. Usually it meant dropping by some-one's home just to talk. Many good memories of those visits remain from past years.

If chatting with others is something you like, you should attend the daily gathering at the Cloudcroft post office, Monday through Friday, 10 AM. One person I regularly saw there was Joseph Ziegenfuss of the Silver Cloud subdivision. Joe and a brother did home repair work. Once they painted a house of mine when I didn't have time myself, and they did a good job.

Joe was always supportive of law enforcement and we had a mutual

liking for cars. I went by his home from time to time and quickly learned he devoted much effort to caring for his elderly parents. His father, Donald, passed away a few years ago. After that Joe continued to look after his mother, Joanne.

Joe cooked and cleaned and obtained medications for his parents and was a good and honorable son. He impressed me with his dedication, always putting his needs behind those of his folks. To me, Joe was a poster boy of that Biblical command: "Honor your mother and your father, that your days may be long." Without a doubt, he honored them.

From visiting their home, I remember his mother, and recall she had a little dog or two that she loved. She and I talked a little. Just a few days ago, I learned of Mrs. Ziegenfuss' death in El Paso this past November 5[th]. I saw that she preferred a donation to your local Humane Society in lieu of flowers.

What an honorable thing to ask for. Flowers are beautiful but temporary and the needs of animals are on-going, permanent. They're dependent on us humans. I'm generally a social person but my pets have always been important to me. Sometimes I prefer their company. They usually just want a warm place to sleep, a little attention, freedom from fleas, something to eat, and water to drink.

My love of animals and particularly dogs began early on. When I was a year old, a little stray terrier mix came to our house. She was also about one year old. My family named her Ears. I was two during 1945 when the U. S. bombing of Japan was taking place. All day long, one heard references to "Tokyo" on the radio.

I was just beginning to talk, and somehow noticed that Ears' prominent ears stood straight up when the word Tokyo was mentioned, so my mother said I began calling her that to watch her ears pop up. Thus she was renamed Tokyo.

Simply speaking, she was a full member of our family for 18 years. She went nearly everywhere with us. Her regular travel place in the car was the shelf under the rear window. At least it was for five years.

In 1950, my parents bought a new Pontiac convertible. I watched when the passenger door was opened to Tokyo the first time, as she bounded into the back seat area to take her usual spot. But there was a cavity behind the back seat for the convertible top to drop into. She tumbled into that hole unexpectedly, scrambled out with a natural sense of survival, and from that moment, decided that a spot on the back seat would be better. Even in later cars with a rear window shelf, she never returned to that perch. "Fool me once…" I suppose she thought.

She was my sleeping companion when I was a child, and I don't mean on the foot of the bed. Tokyo's head rested on the pillow. If the weather was cold, she shared the blanket. Our family moved to Oregon, traveling almost 3,000 miles in a 1955 Ford when I was 12, and she and I and the television set were the back seat passengers. Even Richard the parrot rode up front with my mother, my brother and my sister.

At 18, old for any dog, Tokyo was deaf and blind, her systems were shutting down, and no other choice seemed possible other than to have her euthanized. She seemingly refused to die of her own accord. To this day, when I pass the building that formerly housed a veterinarian's office in Zachary, Louisiana, where her life ended, I think of her and that event.

Tokyo's influence on my life led me to have other similarly dedicated family pets…Snowball, Killer, Bantam, Cookie, Sara Lee. They stayed for their lifetime, with the exception of Sara Lee who was adopted by a Sacramento Mountain family who'd kept her as I traveled extensively. She has a great home and loves the mountains.

The author, age two, with his dog Tokyo, in Liberty, Mississippi, 1945.

Cookie, a mixed Lab, spent 10 of her 12 years in Cloudcroft, and became an occasional visitor to the Boardwalk, though that was against the rules. She relished the attention she got. She liked to rescue drowning golf balls from the pond on the Lodge course and was taken into custody there twice, and I had to bail her out. She loved to walk the trails with us, and to help gather Christmas trees. Some of Cookie's ashes are scattered along her favorite routes.

With the exception of Bantam, our purebred Doberman, all our dogs were strays/mixed breeds, which in my opinion often make the best pets. They'll trade a lot of love for just a little in return. The needs for such animals are practically endless.

Thanks, Mrs. Ziegenfuss, for your unselfish request that caused me to remember these things. In Otero County, her wish may be fulfilled by

a donation to the Otero County Animal Shelter at 601 Wright Avenue in Alamogordo NM 88310. The caring manager, Ms. Lori Soto, says they welcome dog and cat food, as well as cash. Pedigree brand food is preferred, in both adult and puppy versions. As many as 80 dogs are kept, and volunteers are always welcome to walk the animals while staff cleans their runs and cages. The needs are nearly endless. Call the shelter at 575-434-2959 for more details.

My sympathy to Joe Ziegenfuss and his family for the loss of their mother. Rest in peace, ma'am, and help us keep a safe watch on the beautiful creatures that make our lives better on this earth.

55

Protecting and Serving, 24/7. Who You Gonna Call, Ghostbusters?

February 2015

Police officers are taking a serious hit in the national media. Be careful what you believe!

The game plan for television reporters? Start with general assignments. Develop a reputation for unusual stories, things that excite and stir the mud, get people worked up. Get a weekend desk assignment as a part-time talking head.

Become a full-time anchor. Set your sights on a CNN job. Excite, promote, achieve. Make the big bucks. Use social media to the max. Have the killer clothes, the killer body, be popular.

There's always a current "issue", someone to attack. Pick the easy targets, the ones that can't defend themselves too readily or easily. Cops are always handy.

What was the most worrisome thing in our world just five months ago?

Ebola. It was the threat, the scourge of the inter-planetary system. And today? Ho hum. Nobody talks about it. We sent nearly 3,000 U. S. troops to Liberia and forgot they were there. The talking heads and the news directors quickly tired of Ebola.

Motivated many years ago by the chance to be involved in police aviation, I joined a very large police department. Quickly I learned that everyday police work was an honorable – sometimes exciting – fun – job in which to further my life's goals. It was a way to matter, to help people. In short, I liked it.

Did I see corruption? The first time someone tried to corrupt me was with a folded $20 bill attached to a driver's license. It came from a citizen, not a police officer.

I found that the great majority of cops were honest. I learned that the people who disliked the bad apples the most were the overwhelming number of good apples.

A few times, I encountered officers who were dishonest. We weeded them out. We were trusted with people's things in the still of the night, and there was no place for a thief.

Who do you blame for the bad ones you read about? There are no magic gardens where baby police candidates are grown. They come from society. They were and are your sons – daughters – neighbors – cousins. As society degenerates, so does the pool from which successful applicants come.

Do you experience cops who are badge-heavy? When we interviewed potential recruits, the ones who concerned us were the ones who "always wanted to be a cop". Who in their right mind would want what police officers are experiencing just now, and to an extent, even then? We'd rather find a guy or gal who had common sense, who cared about people in general, who just needed a job.

I was a substation commander, with 200 cops in my district. I had three bad ones. Two were ushered out the door. The third, a legal beagle, proved more difficult to rid ourselves of. So we neutralized him by keeping him in a job away from the public.

Of the remaining 197, I saw a group of 30 organize into a Christmas caroling group to visit hospitals, nursing homes, schools – on their off-duty time. For years, Officer Ralph Garcia of the San Antonio, Texas, Police Department worked hard to obtain turkeys and all the trimmings to annually feed the poor at Thanksgiving, as Deputy Sheriff Wally Anderson of the Otero County Sheriff's Office did to gather Christmas Toys for Tots here in Alamogordo.

Many of the poor children in our area of San Antonio, Texas, actually thought Santa wore a blue suit, not a red one, since our station's Blue Santa was the only one they ever saw.

Was singing all our Christmas carolers did? One of our singers, Officer Anthony Linson, a young black man, was with me when we encountered a man holding a shotgun to the head of an infant. He offered himself up to save the child's life and it worked, the most courageous act I witnessed during my police career during which the officer lived.

This past Christmas, my son, who heads a small task force in Texas in his 18th year of policing, helped break up an international ring of thieves, recovering more than $60,000 of stolen property in just one day, much of it taken from mall parking lots. People got their things back. He and his officers worked through the holiday. I know because I met him out and about on Christmas Eve. More than 50 officers were involved.

During the same time, one officer – a bad apple – took $7,000 from a drug dealer, and was caught. What story "trended" on social media? The latter, naturally. Who figured it out, who corrected it? The good apples, of course.

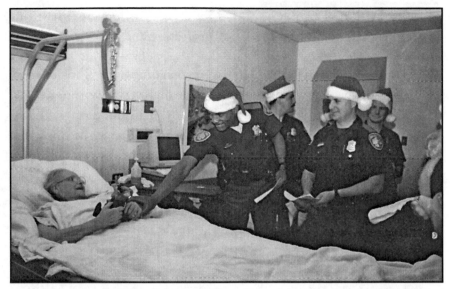

At Christmas 1996, officers of the San Antonio, Texas, Police Department offer best wishes!

Police officers do make mistakes in dealing with the public. Too often they keep to themselves. Too often they stay in their car or pickup when they should be out talking to you, interacting. During police cadet training, some of the best advice I ever got was from a Detective Tony Montalvo. "Hang out with everyday people. Don't spend all your off-duty time with other cops, which will be a tempting thing to do. Keep a balanced view of life," he told us, correctly.

Some departments are now installing windows so tinted – in violation of even state law which restricts citizens as to how "dark" a window can be – that we cannot even see who or what is driving a police vehicle. Though it might give some protection from a sniper, it's the wrong approach. Is it Robocop? Is it a man or woman, my neighbor, a young officer from my church, inside? I want to know. I want to wave at them, make eye contact.

Lately, I've actually seen a few stories where good things that cops have done are shown. Why? It seemed to start happening just after

the assassination of two New York City officers, who were just sitting inside their car, doing nothing – but protecting and serving.

When things go bump in the night, who you gonna call? Ghostbusters? No, it will be the cop who went to work at 11 PM, or went to sleep at 11 PM, being on call and responding when that phone rings. It'll be the guy or gal who is nice to old people, who will never be known as Mr. Popularity because he or she arrested someone's friend or family member for DWI, family violence, or wrote them a traffic ticket.

It will be the young man or woman wearing a badge who picked up a stray dog and couldn't stand to take it to the animal pound and took it home instead and keeps it in the back yard.

It will be a person who will help you, whether they're your friend or not.

"Blessed are the peacemakers…" says the Bible, Jesus' words. Trust me on this…cops spend a lot more time promoting peace than doing other things.

You can help. Next time you see the guys or gals at the coffee shop, just tell them: "Hey, I appreciate what you do." They're not the enemy, and you'd be surprised to learn just how welcome that will be right now.

56

In April, Thoughts Turn to Flights of Fancy in a Cloudzoni 101

April 2015

It may be a surprise to learn that Cloudcroft has a mostly secret airport, not far from the village. Sort of our own Area 51.

In aviation lingo, El Paso is ELP. Albuquerque is ABQ. Since someone once flew from here to Mexico, we're known as CIA, Cloudcroft International Airport. Somehow that identifier seems appropriate for a clandestine flying field operation.

If you're a skeptic and don't believe that CIA exists, may we agree that it's a pretend airport for the sake of this story? Thanks.

Most aviators here own and operate the Cloudzoni 101, a high-wing aircraft much like the old reliable Cessna 172 in design, but higher in performance for our thinner air at almost 9,000 feet above sea level. Like its distant non-flying cousin, the Zamboni, it's a machine that will smooth out a rough ride over places with snow and ice underneath.

Sacramento Mountain folk aren't stupid when it comes to aviation matters. To prove it, here are 10 flight-related questions, and an extra bonus one. You're on the honor system since the answers follow, but I'm pretty sure I can trust you. You get three guesses at each question and the first two guesses don't count. Successfully answering the bonus question earns double credit.

Okay, here we go. Hands on the throttle…

1. Donna and Jim, two Cloudcroft residents, departed CIA in their Cloudzoni 101 for Las Vegas (NV) for Spring Break. There'd been only 20 minutes of fuel in the plane, just enough to get to Alamogordo, but before leaving CIA they topped off the tanks. The trip is 1,000 miles and the airplane will use 10 gallons of fuel per hour at 100 MPH. The aircraft holds 60 gallons. How long can they fly before refueling?

2. Once a local pilot had lost his aeronautical map and while following the highway up "the hill", sheared the wings off his aircraft. Where did the accident happen?

3. A Texas pilot flew a very fast Lone Star BroncBuster X19 race plane on just the reverse course, but was alert and bypassed the obstacle posed by the last question. Impatient, he flew haphazardly around every Cloudcroft pilot who was on his or her way to Walmart, but the locals overtook him anyway. Where did they catch up?

4. A Cloudzoni 777, the large commercial version, was flying to Colorado with an 800 pound load of legal marijuana. The aircraft was identified with WWII nose art as the "Mary Jane". One pilot had to make an emergency bathroom stop, so they landed at CIA. It takes less distance to land an airplane than to get it airborne. The runway was too short for a takeoff so the load had to be lightened. Cloudcroft citizens, always good about volunteering, stepped forward to guard the aircraft overnight. How much lighter was the Mary Jane when it made a good takeoff the next day?

5. An enterprising Cloudcroft businessman/pilot successfully bid on the U. S. Postal route from Alamogordo to Cloudcroft – he would ferry the mail in his Cloudzoni - but later lost the contract in a lawsuit in federal court. The holder of the current delivery method alleged discrimination and proved it. What issue did he successfully litigate?

6. What creative but low cost safety device, designed by the village council, allows all pilots who operate out of CIA to know they're safe?

7. What well-known personality set the Around-The-World Non-Stop flight record from Cloudcroft in a Cloudzoni 101 during 2003, while blind-folded and strapped into his seat upside-down?

8. Why is it impossible to fly from Cloudcroft to Artesia non-stop, just 80 air miles?

9. Not counting the limiting factors in question # 8, another hazard to aviation exists on that route so that a Cloudzoni cruising at 100 MPH which should be able to cover those 80 miles in 8/10 of an hour or 48 minutes, usually takes 51 minutes. What causes that extra delay?

10. The Cloudzoni 101 is actually a great investment, in that local owners selling a used, worn-out one always get more than their original cost back. Why is that?

11. Bonus Question…ref question # 1. Donna and Jim filled up with some real aviation fuel in Alamogordo and arrived in Las Vegas. On return, while over Tularosa, they noticed rumbling storm clouds completely blanketing Cloudcroft. A howling late spring snowstorm was in progress. In fact it was a blizzard with complete white-out conditions. No aviation light known to mankind was bright enough so that it might be spotted through the weather in order to land safely. All their training said: Do a 180 degree turn, avoid the problem, land in Alamo. But they were anxious to be back for Moose Club night and agreed that

one dazzling beacon of hope did exist in the village which would allow them to vector from it to the airport and survive. What was it?

Well, how did you do? If you scored less than 30%, you don't have enough common sense to live in Cloudcroft. Move immediately to Santa Fe or Taos.

And look upwards and give thanks for living in our beautiful village with its old-world-charm airport, the one where stairs are still rolled out to the planes. Have a great April Fool's Day as well!

Answers:

1. Only 20 minutes. The fuel at a pretend airport isn't real and won't get you anywhere. Remember, you just agreed.

2. Going through the tunnel.

3. Over the stoplight on U. S. 82 at Highway 54/70.

4. 840 lbs. They also siphoned five gallons of fuel out of one of the tanks, at 8 lbs per gallon.

5. Cruelty to Animals. The owner said the donkey's family suffered when the donkey on the route lost its job.

6. In the operations shack, pilots must log each take-off on a chalkboard, then log each landing on return. If the numbers are equal, the pilot knows he or she is safe.

7. NBC news anchor Brian Williams.

8. Have to land at the fruit stand. Also acceptable: Have to pull

over past Mayhill at MM37 or at the Hope roadside park east of that town to pee on the ground.

9. Must slow down over Hope or risk getting a speeding ticket.

10. They're sold as "better than new" by auctioneer Carl Wood.

11. The Family Dollar sign.

57

You've Gotta Know When to Hold 'em, Know When to Fold 'em...

June 2015

Since June 2006, this column appeared monthly in the Cloudcroft newspaper, The Mountain Monthly. It began from a small cell in Santa Fe's maximum security prison. If you've been a regular reader, you weren't last month, since a story wasn't here. Circumstances simply prevented it being posted.

Yes, 2015 marks nine years! About halfway along, one other month was skipped, just a miscommunication. These little adventures have often been submitted during a road trip, even from public library computers. A small labor, perhaps, but a labor of love.

In the Bible, the Good Lord promises us three score and ten. At 72, I'm already on borrowed time. My hope is to keep my credit in good standing and borrow more. But as Kenny Rogers sang..."You gotta know when to hold 'em, know when to fold 'em...". So for these stories, it's folding time.

Never expecting to write this long, I finally made a vague goal of

keeping up the chatter for a decade. Being a 90 percenter has usually satisfied me, though, and so be it. I am truly humbled to have been here this long, to think that anyone would really care what I had to say.

Thank you, good readers!

You've patiently indulged or at least tolerated a variety of subjects… some serious, some not so. A major purpose has been to remind you of what Deputy Bob Hedman gave us on December 18, 2004…his life. Please don't forget him. I visit his family annually in New York State. They're doing well. His mother, now 80, has just finished treatment for cancer, and thus far it's a success story.

Is the supply of stories exhausted? No. There are many issues that concern me. One is the hammer that police officers find themselves under. The guys and gals I know work hard for you. For every unfortunate misdeed, there are thousands of good ones, daily. Very few professions come into contact with so many who need help, and any cop with a good heart cannot turn away. Law enforcement seeks those with good hearts. I really liked my job, and it was a special opportunity to help others, to matter. It was an honor to serve you.

Sure, next thing I'll be seeking is world peace, right? Good luck to us on that!

But travel, at least the low-budget variety, occupies my thoughts. I haven't adopted the Harvey Hardy Method yet, but may be getting close. So little time, so much to see. And that's just in the lower 48 of the United States. I have dreams of visiting mainland Europe – Alaska – Canada to include the Calgary Stampede – of a return trip to Honduras where I spent a small part of my youth. A Mississippi River adventure may finally happen in the next year or so.

Attorney Harvey Hardy died at age 93 in San Antonio, Texas, in July 2008. He was the son of two lawyers, and was self-taught, having

challenged and passed the Texas bar exam without having attended law school. He was a conscientious, honorable man. At 90, he came roaring into Cloudcroft, driven by a nephew. We had lunch at the Aspen Café. I gave him the nickel tour, which lasted all of 10 minutes before he departed in a cloud of dust.

"I don't have much time, and I want to visit all the places I always longed to, and never did," he said, "and now I've seen this one."

Personally, I haven't seen enough of Cloudcroft, but I did get his drift. The Harvey Hardy Method.

To the current and former staff of the Mountain Monthly, thank you for allowing me to waste so many good trees. You've been great!

An apology is due for one unfilled promise. In April 2013, I ventured to write a travelogue for RVs on U. S. Highway 82 for its 1,700 mile length from Alamogordo – featuring Cloudcroft, naturally - to Brunswick, Georgia, where it ends at Interstate 95, just six miles from the Atlantic Ocean.

That journey was taken over two weeks, traveling from sunup to sundown, then working on research for the next day's portion, usually until midnight. Only the middle Sunday was idle time, for laundry and such. But my coverage was incomplete (at that end of that "vacation", a rest was necessary), and a westbound trip is needed to finish up. Plans are in the works.

I'll stay in touch with my Cloudcroft friends, and welcome new e-mails to BillyAndersNM@aim.com. Provide enough detail in the subject line so I know you aren't Sammie Spam. Please check my website www. BillyAndersAuthor.com for books that feature the village.

Back to our Bible. The book of Ecclesiastes tells us there is a right time for everything. In part, it says...

"There is a time to be born. And there's a time to die… There is a time to weep. And there's a time to laugh.

There is a time to be sad. And there's a time to dance…There is a time to be silent. And there's a time to speak. There is a time to love…"

Thank you for the love, and the time you gave me to speak. I hope I had the good sense to know when to be silent. A valiant attempt was made to maximize laugh time, and keep the negatives to a minimum.

You are appreciated. Cloudcroft and the Sacramento Mountain area are truly a little bit of heaven. God bless each of you, and see you on the Boardwalk!

My wife, me, and our oldest son, Brett, during 1998 in one of our favorite places, downtown Cloudcroft!

Epilogue

Our involvement with the Cloudcroft area of New Mexico has now lasted more than 20 years. That's at the top end of time spent by "non-locals". It's a special place, a blue-collar sort of special place. If you're interested in helping maintain that, remember it isn't what you did before you got here that's so important as what you do after you arrive.

The only permanent thing in the world is change, which is inevitable. The nature of Cloudcroft is slowly changing. Twenty years ago, it was unthinkable we might have a "dollar store". But in 2015, it's here. It was hard to believe the little football field next to the high school along U. S. Highway 82 wouldn't be lit up on Friday nights, but now the field is gone and that spot is dark.

The truth is…if we went back and looked in the mirror in 20 year chunks, we'd most likely find reflections of our attitudes about change in those same chunk-sized segments. Anyone who last visited Cloudcroft 40 years ago would be very surprised today. Just remember what you liked about the village when you arrived, and within reason

keep it the same way for future generations. Just because something was done a certain way back in Megapolis doesn't mean it's right here.

The demands of aging – family responsibilities - "back home", plus the desire to travel, limit many of us to some finite period of full-time Cloudcroft involvement, usually between 10 to 20 years. My wife and I have reached that point, but continue to take every opportunity to enjoy cool mountain mornings, to sip hot coffee or hot chocolate while the winter snow gently falls, to consider the deer or elk in our yard as friends and not as a food source. We love New Mexico.

So relax...turn your car alarm off...and enjoy not stopping at a stop-light. Treat water as a limited precious resource, which it is. If you're able to live in the Sacramento Mountains for a number of years as we have, or better yet a lifetime, you're a lucky rascal!

CPSIA information can be obtained at www.ICGtesting.com
Printed in the USA
LVOW10s1153020116

468693LV00003B/5/P